Chambers
BOOK OF TENNIS FACTS

Swayam Ganguly is a Kolkata-based author, editorial consultant, and sports enthusiast. His sports books include *Chambers Book of Football Facts*, *Chambers Book of Cricket Facts*, and *Gukesh Dommaraju: From Chess Prodigy to World Champion.* Passionate storytelling, emotional richness, and the use of playful puns make his works stand out. A huge tennis buff, he grew up watching legends like Boris Becker and Steffi Graf, among others. When he is not writing, he directs corporate films.

Chambers BOOK OF TENNIS FACTS

SWAYAM GANGULY

hachette INDIA

First published in paperback in 2026 by Hachette India
(Registered name: Hachette Book Publishing India Pvt. Ltd)
An Hachette UK company
www.hachetteindia.com

1

ISBN 978-93-5731-830-3

Hachette Book Publishing India Pvt. Ltd
4th & 5th Floors, Corporate Centre,
Plot No. 94, Sector 44, Gurugram 122003, India

Typeset in Sabon 11/14.2
by InoSoft Systems, Noida

Printed and bound in India
by Manipal Technologies Limited

MIX
Paper | Supporting responsible forestry
FSC™ C043100
FSC
www.fsc.org

To my sister-in-law, Reema Ganguly,
who never misses a Grand Slam

CONTENTS

PREFACE

Of fine margins and timeless moments, tennis is a sport where a single point can alter history and a single match can redefine greatness. From sunlit grass courts to gruelling baseline battles, the game has evolved across eras, yet its essence remains unchanged: precision, endurance, and an unyielding will to win.

Chambers Book of Tennis Facts is an invitation to step into this fascinating world – not just as a spectator but as an informed enthusiast. It brings together the structure of the sport – its rules, formats, and tournaments – with the stories and statistics that have shaped its legacy. From the classical dominance of Björn Borg and the fiery genius of John McEnroe to the trailblazing courage of Billie Jean King – whose iconic 'Battle of the Sexes' against Bobby Riggs redefined the cultural landscape of sport – this book is also an attempt to honour the figures who shaped tennis beyond the court.

It journeys through the grandeur of the four Grand Slams – Wimbledon Championships, French Open, US

Open, and Australian Open – while celebrating eras of brilliance, from Steffi Graf to Serena Williams and the defining modern rivalry of Roger Federer, Rafael Nadal, and Novak Djokovic.

What sets this volume apart is its commitment to both depth and discovery. Beyond milestone records and statistics, it offers an interactive experience where QR codes connect you directly to some of the best moments of the sport. As every page reveals a new layer of the game, readers do not just read through, they also relive some of the finest moments in world tennis.

Designed for fans, learners, sports aficionados, and quiz enthusiasts alike, this book is more than a repository of facts – it is a full-blown extravaganza just as the game is.

Step on to the court. The game awaits!

INTRODUCTION

Today, all four Grand Slam tournaments are money-making blockbusters, which is evident from the overnight queues for the expensive tickets and the surge in television viewership. The Wimbledon Championships alone generated more than half a billion dollars in revenue in 2024–25. This is remarkable for a tournament that lasts for only two weeks. Tennis is a grand spectacle today, both on and off the court. If the superstars battling it out like gladiators armed with tennis rackets, which have replaced swords, aren't enough, the kings and queens who serve as the audience of the sport also grab eyeballs. From Hollywood stars to the rich and famous to fashion icons to sports stars from other fields, they are all present in the stands, dressed in their resplendent best and rooting for their favourite players. Tennis viewership, especially for Grand Slams like Wimbledon, has witnessed a significant surge in recent years. The substantial rise has been observed both in terms of television and digital viewership. In India, for example, Wimbledon viewership catapulted to a staggering 176% in 2024. The Broadcast Audience Research Council (BARC) India data revealed that a total of 36.3 million viewers watched the Wimbledon Championships. Although football, cricket, and basketball have comparatively larger global fan bases, tennis enjoys a wide fan base in the Americas, Europe, and Asia. Countries like France, Australia, and Switzerland reflect a strong regional fan base. The pace at which the tennis market is growing exponentially is especially encouraging for tennis lovers. It is expected that the tennis industry will increase from 7.86 billion USD to 13.24 billion USD by 2032. Tennis as a sport ranks third in viewership among all non-cricket sports on the basis of linear television viewership in India. Game, set, and match to tennis fans! This compendium is for all of them!

1

THE HISTORY OF TENNIS

The discovery of tennis can be traced back to 12th-century France. The game was originally played by monks to relax from their holy schedules during ceremonial occasions. The sport was played just like a handball game, which was called palm or 'paume' or 'jeu de paume' or 'the game of the palm'. The monks played this game by hitting a ball back and forth, but using the palms of their hands to do so. In time, a black leather glove was used to cover the hand. This is understandable as the monks must have had trouble with ceremonial work that demanded the use of their hands. Hitting the ball with the palm continuously can be quite painful at times. This was especially true for the French monks as the original tennis balls were quite different from the ones used now.

THE HISTORY OF THE TENNIS BALL

According to the International Tennis Federation (ITF), the weight of a tennis ball must be between 56.0 and 59.4 grams. A tennis ball must be between 2.5 and 2.8 inches in diameter.

The French villagers who fashioned the first tennis ball were not subjected to such rigid requirements. They made their ball by using wool, putty, hair, and wood. During the early days of tennis, the first balls that evolved from the woollen balls used by the monks were made of leather and stuffed with wool or fur and sometimes even with cloth and string. Tennis balls were also made with feathers that were wrapped in strips of cloth or textile strips that were sewn together with thread and then filled with feathers. These heavy balls didn't bounce as much as desired. It wasn't until much later that a cellulose material was used to make the balls bounce much better. Today, tennis balls are made by combining rubber and felt. It was only in the 1870s that the first rubber tennis balls were invented, which were made up of felt-coated hollow vulcanized rubber.

The Yellow Tennis Ball

The year 1972 saw the introduction of the yellow tennis ball by Mike Davies. Before this, tennis balls were predominantly white, which caused visibility issues on a tennis court. This led to the introduction of the optic yellow ball so that both the players and the spectators would be able to sight the ball properly, especially those watching the matches on television. Wimbledon first introduced yellow balls in 1986.

The history of tennis balls dates back to the very history of the sport itself, and the tennis ball has been a constant companion of the tennis player over the long years. Interestingly, these tennis balls are changed now after every nine games have concluded in a tennis match. The only exception is when a tiebreaker is on when the ball change is delayed till the first game of a new set begins. The reason for the ball change is that tennis balls are subject to immense pounding and hammering, so much so that they have a limited shelf life after the ball can has been unsealed. Apart from the heavy pounding unleashed so forcefully on these balls, they are also weather sensitive. If a tennis ball gets a little wet, it loses its bounce forever and becomes useless in a tennis match. Now you know why they don't play tennis in the rain. New balls, please!

THE ORIGIN OF THE NAME

The game of jeu de paume was so infectious that it spread all over Europe as all the monks started playing and enjoying it. The game of tennis evolved gradually into a proper sport in Europe and beyond. It is interesting to note how tennis derived its name from the Anglo–Norman term 'tenez'. When the French monks started playing the game in the 12th century, they used to throw and catch a ball while shouting 'tenez', which basically means to take heed.

Take This!

The French word 'tenez' is the formal form of the French verb 'tenir', which basically means 'to hold'.

It's common to say, 'Here you go', 'There you go', 'Here you are', 'Take this', or 'Take that'. In tennis, this command was shouted by the server to their opponent. 'Tenez' is also used as an expression of surprise to mean 'Hey!' or 'How about that!'

THE FIRST KEY ERA IN TENNIS HISTORY

When tennis began in the monastic cloisters of northern France, the rules were as simple as life in the monastery. There were no umpires, no rackets, and almost no rules at all. All the players did was knock the ball back and forth with their hands in outdoor spaces.

The jeu de paume was the first key era in tennis history and lasted from the 12th to the 16th centuries. The predecessor to modern tennis, it witnessed the first evolution of the sport with gloves being introduced, followed by rackets.

THE EVOLUTION OF THE TENNIS RACKET

For greater convenience, the monks also decided to add a handle to the black leather glove they had added earlier to the game of jeu de paume. Those hard balls must have hurt those delicate monkish hands. Sure enough, players in the 12th century suffered from red and swollen hands playing the 'game of the palm'. This led to some serious thought, and that's how the world's first tennis racquet or racket originated. However, proper rackets were only introduced in the 16th century, when the game evolved to what we know and see today. Interestingly, the word racket takes its name from the Arabic word 'rakhat', which means the palm of the hand.

The early forms of tennis rackets were simple paddles that came to be used in real tennis. The modern tennis racket we see today is the result of years of technological advancement. The earliest tennis rackets were made of wood, with animal gut strings to strike the ball. The design of this pre-19th-century tennis racket was ridiculously simple, with a long handle and a small, usually lopsided head that was designed to reach those low-bouncing balls of real tennis.

Wooden rackets arrived on the scene and ruled the roost from the 19th century to the mid-20th century. The simple wooden rackets witnessed a massive transformation during this era as their heads became larger and more symmetrical for ease of play. Wooden racket manufacturers like Slazenger, Dunlop, Spalding, and Wilson made a name for themselves with key improvements made in lamination and string technology. The Dunlop Maxply Fort and the Wilson Jack Kramer were the most preferred rackets of this era. But the problem with wooden rackets was that they were heavy and cumbersome for a strenuous game like tennis. Lighter rackets seemed to be the order of the day. The metal and composite rackets used presently in tennis were first introduced in the mid-20th century. In fact, the beginning of 1967 saw the introduction of metal rackets when Wilson Sporting Goods made a metal racket for tennis. Prior to this, wooden frames were used to fashion tennis rackets. However, the first attempts to introduce metal frames to tennis rackets were met with complaints of vibration and string damage. This was worked upon and improved, and in the 1960s, a durable steel racket called the Wilson T2000 became very popular in tennis circles because it offered more power. In 1968, Spalding launched an aluminium racket called 'The Smasher', which did justice to its name. In time, other materials were developed, like carbon fibre and other composites, to make tennis rackets both lightweight and powerful. Modern rackets today often boast of oversized heads with wider frames and have been created with advanced materials, such as graphite, to give the players the luxury of a better performance. However, the overall length permitted for a tennis racket is restricted to 29 inches. Today, modern rackets have the luxury of being created with carbon fibre, graphite, and several metals to grant the professional tennis player mastery over the game in terms of power, manoeuvrability, and control. The primitivism of the wooden racket has been replaced by a wide variety of grips and stances adopted by modern tennis players. Each style, right from the continental to the eastern, the semi-western to the western grips, adds a different layer and dimension to the game. Each has a varying level of torso rotation that adds more power to those strokes. The evolution of the tennis racket is a shining example of the human quest to seek perfection in sport.

Did You Know?

The strings or guts of the tennis racket were once made out of the guts of cows and sheep.

RACKET OR RACQUET?

'Racket' is commonly used to spell the device used to play tennis. The alternative spelling, 'racquet', is also used but is common in other sports like racketball or squash. However, the United States Tennis Association (USTA), which is a non-profit organization with the goal of promoting and developing tennis in the USA, uses 'racquet' as the spelling for lawn tennis.

Tennis Balls and Rackets

BJÖRN BORG'S LOVE AFFAIR WITH WOOD

The name that instantly springs to mind when one talks about wooden tennis rackets is Swedish legend Björn Borg. He preferred playing with the Donnay Allwood and Bancroft models of wooden rackets when he dominated tennis in the 1970s and early 1980s. The first one helped him win his five consecutive Wimbledon titles. Borg's weapons of war were classic wooden laminated rackets that had an oval head and a concave throat. When Borg made a comeback from his retirement, he tried using a modern graphite racket. But he was visibly uncomfortable and started using a wooden racket again, despite the vast advancements made by tennis technology.

THE ICE MAN IN TENNIS HISTORY

When we discuss the male GOATs of tennis history today, the names that crop up instantly are the Big Three of male tennis – Roger Federer, Rafael Nadal, and Novak Djokovic, along with Serena Williams in women's tennis. Also, Carlos Alcaraz and Jannik Sinner are the modern-day greats dominating tennis today. While it is true that all these tennis players have outstanding achievements to their names to rise to the very top, one tennis player stands apart silently.

Swedish tennis legend Björn Borg was an icon during his playing career. Many fans believe that Borg was the greatest player of all time because of his stellar achievements during a relatively brief career. Consider this: 11 Grand Slam Singles titles comprising 6 French Open titles and 5 consecutive Wimbledon wins. His career is especially extraordinary if one considers that Borg was just 20 years old when he won his first French Open title and retired at 26. Furthermore, few players in tennis history can match his ability to triumph on both clay and grass, two vastly different surfaces. This was especially revolutionary in the era Borg played in. If you consider the Big Three in recent times, only Rafael Nadal dominated on clay, which is a fair assessment of how tough it is to win on both surfaces as a tennis player.

However, critics argue that Borg's inability to win the US Open and the Australian Open is what does not make him the GOAT of tennis, especially as the Big Three (Federer, Nadal, and Djokovic) have all won a Career Grand Slam by winning all the Grand Slam tournaments at least once.

Also, the argument is that Borg's career lacked the longevity desired for GOAT status as he retired at the tender age of 26. But who knows what would have happened if Borg had decided to play on? In his defence, he had an 89% win rate in Grand Slam matches and an overall 82.7% win rate. Björn Borg was also the first man in the Open Era to win 10 Grand Slam titles.

Björn Borg

Borg's ability to remain calm under pressure earned him the nickname 'The Ice Man'. His two-handed backhands and topspin-heavy ground strokes were ahead of their time. His baseline play helped formulate modern tennis strategies. Björn Borg was not without his rivals, which included big names like John McEnroe and Jimmy Connors. The 1980 Wimbledon final between Borg and McEnroe is considered one of the greatest matches in tennis history.

Björn Borg vs John McEnroe | Wimbledon 1980 Final | Full Match

Björn Borg returned to professional tennis in 1991, after a retirement that lasted eight years. But obviously, the magic was not there anymore, and he struggled to regain his earlier form. Borg made a final retirement from tennis after two years of his comeback. His return was brief, just like his stellar career. Unlike Björn Borg, no professional player uses a wooden tennis racket anymore. In fact, the best tennis players in the world prefer to get their rackets custom-made to their precise specifications and preferences.

Let's take a look at the rackets used by the Big Three and the she-GOAT of tennis for a better understanding.

Player	Racket	Head Size	Strung Weight
Roger Federer	Wilson Pro Staff RF97	97 sq. inches	12.6 ounces
Rafael Nadal	Babolat Pure Aero	100 sq. inches	11.3 ounces
Novak Djokovic	Head Graphene 360+ Speed Pro	95 sq. inches	12.7 ounces
Serena Williams	Wilson Blade SW104 Autograph	104 sq. inches	11.4 ounces

THE EARLY TENNIS SHOES

In 1892, the first tennis shoes were invented and named plimsolls. These early tennis shoes were made of cloth with rubber buttons. Initially, these shoes were designed and manufactured for the British Navy to wear on the decks of their ships. Because these shoes made no sound while walking, they were also given the moniker sneakers. At the time, there was no right or left shoe. The plimsolls remained a popular style till the 1960s, until advanced versions of tennis shoes from different brands emerged in the market. Keds is the oldest brand of tennis shoes, which arrived in the USA in 1916. Keds became a popular shoe to wear while playing tennis. Keds was created by the United States Rubber Company, which was later renamed Uniroyal. In 1917, Converse released the All-Star tennis shoe, but Adidas released the first sneaker exclusively for tennis in 1931.

LOVE ALL

Most of us know that each game in tennis comprises points: 15, 30, and 40. This scoring system might seem complicated to a layman, especially because all other sports have preferred to keep their scoring systems rather simple in comparison.

The scoring system of tennis also originated in medieval France, when a clock face was utilized to display the scores. The hand of the clock was moved to the next quarter for every point scored, and that explains the origin of the points 15, 30, and 45. The first player to reach 60 was the winner of the game, and that concluded the game.

The concept of 'deuce' was also added so that a player could not win a game with a one-point differential in player scores. The 45 on the clock was thus changed to 40 to keep the score inside the 60 ticks on the clock face. So, if both players were on 40 points, the first player to score received 10 points, which brought the clock to 50. If the player on 50 scored again, they were rewarded with 10 more points, and the clock was reset to 60 seconds. 60 signalled the end of the game.

Another theory is that because players had to win by 2 points, the hand of the clock was moved to 40 and then to 50, with the win arriving on the hour mark. The third theory or explanation suggests that the scoring system was devised keeping in mind the number of yards the tennis ball travelled. In those early days, the courts were only

90 yards in length, with 45 yards of width each side. Every time a player scored a point, the players moved forward by 15 feet. When the third point was eventually scored in the game, both players were standing up at the net. The final point of the game was made only at a distance of 10 yards. Cut to the tennis courts today, where such a rule is non-existent, thankfully, with each court boasting a standard measurement of 78 feet in length.

The term 'love all' denotes that both the players in the case of Singles, and both the teams in the case of Doubles, have a score of zero when the game or match begins. The term 'love' in this case is not an English word, which the English conveniently never mention. It originated from the French word 'l'œuf', which means 'egg'. This word, when written, interestingly, resembles the number zero, and was hence bestowed the honour of opening the scoring system in tennis, being the perfect visual representation of zero according to the French. English speakers might have mispronounced this French word and used the term 'love' instead to communicate a zero score in tennis. Well, now you know, love!

THE SECOND KEY ERA IN TENNIS HISTORY

The second key area in tennis history lasted from the 16th century to the 19th century and is known as Real Tennis or Royal Tennis. This was the evolution of jeu de paume to a complex indoor game played with rackets. Real Tennis became an accepted form of sport among European royalty, where tennis was played by royals in enclosed courts with proper equipment. That's why it's also called Royal Tennis.

TENNIS ROYALE

Tennis as a sport has always been linked to royalty, with kings and queens taking to the sport like fish to water. Royalty and wealthy members of society were the ones to play tennis in its early years. This tradition still holds good as tennis is patronized by both royals and wealthy benefactors. King Henry VIII of England was one of the early enthusiasts of the game and a damn fine tennis player, too.

THE FIRST ROYAL TENNIS DEATH

As the game of the palm became famous among French royalty, from just being a monkish sport, King Louis X of France became a big fan and avid player of jeu de paume. He even built several indoor covered courts in Paris at the end of the 13th century after falling in love with this earliest form of tennis. In fact, King Louis hated playing tennis outside in the sun so much that he made tennis an indoor sport for his own playing convenience. But it was his passion that brought about his end.

On an eventful day in June 1316, Louis X decided to shirk his royal duties and spend the day playing tennis instead. After a strenuous game of jeu de paume, the French king made another mistake. He decided to cool down by drinking a large pitcher of cold wine. That ended his reign. The cause of death was most likely pneumonia or pleurisy. There has been a lot of debate over the exact cause of death, and there have been whispers of poisoning. But it's likely that Louis X brought about his own demise. Chilled wine and tennis don't go together unless you are watching the sport, of course. Louis X will always be remembered as the first player in the history of tennis who died after a game.

THE THIRD KEY ERA IN TENNIS HISTORY

The late 19th century was when lawn tennis emerged as the modern game of tennis we know today. It was initially the preferred sport of Victorian gentlemen and ladies, who played on grass courts.

THE TRANSFORMATION: TENNIS TO LAWN TENNIS

But how did tennis transform into its present form of lawn tennis? We have a certain gentleman named Major Walter Clopton Wingfield to thank for that. In December 1873, he invented a version of tennis that players could play outdoors on a lawn. The major named his game 'Sphairistike', which is the Greek term for 'playing ball'. How apt!

The chosen ones were yet again rich folks as the game was played on the Manor House lawn by rich Englishmen and ladies. The court was in the shape of an hourglass. Good old Walter also systemized the game of tennis by inventing a net that was 2 metres high and which divided the tennis court equally. For the first time, tennis began to reflect a look and feel of the game we have all come to watch and love today. If you are still not convinced that Major Walter Clopton Wingfield was not a progressive man, you will be. In 1873, he published the first rules for lawn tennis. He also secured the patent for the game of tennis in February 1874. It did not take much time for the popularity of lawn tennis to go ballistic. While lawn tennis was introduced in the USA in 1874–1875, with first matches being played on grass courts right from 1874 – it was in 1877 that the first lawn tennis tournament in the world took place. It was the inaugural Wimbledon Championship, starting on 9 July 1877, held by the All England Croquet and Lawn Tennis Club.

THE ALL ENGLAND CROQUET CLUB

The Wimbledon district of London, which is famous today for being the oldest and arguably the best Grand Slam in terms of viewership, formed the All England Croquet Club in the late 19th century. When this club was established, it initially focused on the sport of croquet. This was before the invasion of tennis, which completely blew away the sport of croquet thanks to its popularity. The All England Croquet Club embraced lawn tennis, which flourished under its patronage. In 1877, the club hosted a tennis championship that took place in a rectangular court. The rules were the same as modern tennis. After this, the game spread like wildfire to other parts of Britain, and then to America and other parts of the world.

THE FIRST WIMBLEDON CHAMPIONSHIPS

In 1877, the inaugural Wimbledon tournament was held, making it the oldest tennis tournament in history, which is still going strong.

> Spencer Gore became the first Wimbledon champion, defeating William Marshall, 6–1, 6–2, 6–4 in the final to clinch the Gentlemen's Singles tennis title.

Organized by the All England Croquet and Lawn Tennis Club, Wimbledon would go on to become the most prestigious tournament in tennis. When Wimbledon began, it was restricted to only men's Singles. In time, it incorporated other key categories like women's Singles, men's Doubles, women's Doubles, and Mixed Doubles.

THE INAUGURAL US OPEN

After a few years, it was America's turn to jump on the Grand Slam bandwagon. The first US Open was held in 1881. Initially called the US Open Championship, it took place at the Newport Casino in Rhode Island. Richard Sears was the first US Open champion.

THE CHAMPIONNAT DE FRANCE

The first French Open, then known as the Championnat de France, was held in 1891. However, participation in the inaugural edition of the tournament was restricted exclusively to members of French tennis clubs. In a way, it was ironic that the first Singles champion of the French Open was a British tennis player living in Paris at the time. His name was H. Briggs.

Interestingly, the French Open was held in the famous Stade Roland-Garros only in 1928. Prior to that, the tournament was held at various venues, including Île de Puteaux. 1897 saw the French Open welcome women tennis players to participate for the first time.

TENNIS AT THE OLYMPICS

Tennis made its debut in the Olympic Games as early as 1896. Only men were allowed to participate, and John Boland of the USA won the first Olympic gold medal in the men's Singles. In a strange move, tennis was removed from the Olympics after the 1924 Paris Games. This was because of disputes that crept up between the International Lawn Tennis Federation (ILTF) and the International Olympic Committee (IOC) regarding amateurism rules.

The two tennis bodies failed to reach an agreement on how to define and enforce amateur status for tennis players, especially as tennis was becoming more and more professional. One of the major concerns that the ILTF had was that tennis at the Olympics might overshadow Wimbledon. These factors caused the sport's withdrawal from the Olympics. Tennis at the Olympics was not played officially as a sport from 1928 to 1988.

1968 and 1984 witnessed the return of tennis at the Olympics as a demonstration sport. It made a powerful comeback as a full medal sport in the 1988 Seoul Olympics. The return of tennis to the Olympics was thanks largely to the efforts of Juan Antonio Samaranch, then president of the International Olympic Committee. Samaranch insisted that a popular sport like tennis was a must in the Olympic program. Boy, was he right!

THE DAVIS CUP

The turn of the 20th century witnessed the beginning of another great tennis event. In 1900, the first Davis Cup was held, and it was originally known as the International Lawn Tennis Challenge.

Named after American tennis player and philanthropist Dwight Filley Davis, the Davis Cup was initiated by him. He also donated the trophy, and it was only fitting that the Cup be named after him. The Davis Cup became the premier team event for countries in international tennis as a prestigious annual competition between men's national teams. The first Davis Cup face-off was between the USA and Great Britain, who competed as the British Isles. It ended in a surprise victory for Team USA. Since then, a total of 16 countries have won the Davis Cup. The United States has put up a good show after winning the inaugural Davis Cup and has won the most titles, with 32 wins. Australia is a close second with 28 victories.

The Davis Cup has the distinction of being the only international tournament where different countries across the world compete with each other for top honours. Each team has almost six players representing the country. Two players play Singles on a round robin basis, and there are two teams made up of two players each who participate

> The Davis Cup has remained elusive for the Indian tennis team so far. It's been a classic case of so near and yet so far for India, having finished runners-up on as many as three occasions in 1966, 1974, and 1987.

in the Doubles category. Sometimes, a talented player may participate in both the Singles and Doubles categories.

THE FIRST AUSTRALIAN OPEN

The Grand Slam circle was firmly established in tennis with the first Australian Open, held in November 1905. Known as the Australasian Championships then, it was held in the Warehouseman's Cricket Ground in Melbourne. Interestingly, the tournament was a joint venture between Australia and New Zealand. Rodney Heath was the first men's Singles champion. The women's Singles event was included in the Australian Open in 1922.

THE FORMATION OF THE ITF

The ITF, or the International Tennis Federation, was formed on 1 March 1913. This is the international governing body of tennis. The ITF formulates the rules that have to be followed by all the tennis players who take part in tennis competitions across the world. It also sets the guidelines for play, decides upon the kind of equipment that has to be used to play tennis, and sets the court dimensions.

A BRIEF HISTORY OF TENNIS IN INDIA

Tennis became popular in India in the late 19th century, after the British colonial rulers introduced the game to the land. Popular tournaments cropped up, like the Punjab Lawn Tennis Championship in 1885, the Bengal Lawn Tennis Championship in 1887, and the All India Tennis Championships in 1910. These local tournaments were instrumental in making tennis a popular sport in India. In the beginning, British players dominated these tournaments. But slowly and steadily, Indian tennis players like Mohd. Saleem, N.S. Iyer, and Nagu made their mark by registering important wins. 1920 witnessed the formation of the All India Lawn Tennis Association (AILTA), which shaped the structure and eventual growth of tennis in India.

THE TIEBREAK/TIEBREAKER

In tennis, a set is a part of a match that a player must win. There are five sets for men and three sets for women. The player to win three sets first for men and two sets for women is declared the winner of the tennis match.

However, to win a set, a tennis player has to win 6 games. But the catch here is that they need to win these 6 games by at least a 2-game margin. For example, a score of 6–4 or 7–5 is a valid set win. However, a set score of 6–5 is not.

This rule caused a major problem if there was a tie of 6–6 between the two players in a set. The set then continued till a 2-game margin was reached. This often took long hours, and sometimes, days. So, an effective solution had to be reached to break this deadlock. The tiebreaker was invented in 1965 by James Van Alen and solved this problem. Now, if two players were tied in a set at 6–6, a tiebreak or tiebreaker was played to determine the winner of the set.

TIEBREAK RULES

The tiebreak is a sort of mini-match within a tennis match. The first player who reaches 7 points in a tiebreak, with

The Longest Match in a Grand Slam

The record for the longest match in a Grand Slam belongs to John Isner of the USA and Nicolas Mahut of France. At Wimbledon 2010, the two tennis players battled it out for 11 hours and 5 minutes in a marathon match that lasted for 3 days and had to be suspended because of darkness 2 nights in a row. The final set lasted for 8 hours and 11 minutes and is the longest set in tennis history. As many as 123 tennis balls were used in this match. The final score was 6–4, 3–6, 6–7, 7–6, and 70–68. The match went on for so long that the scoreboard ran out of space and had to be manually changed to keep up with the score. The scoreboard became moot – it had a maximum scorekeeping capacity of 47–47, and the score went to 70–68 in the tiebreaker. John Isner emerged as the winner of this marathon tennis match.

a lead of 2 points, is declared the winner of the tiebreak and also the set 7–6.

The players have to continue playing the tiebreak until the 2-point advantage is achieved. There is no limit to how long a tiebreak can continue for a player in the case of Singles. Players in the case of Doubles must win by 2 points.

The tiebreak works on an alternating serve rule. The tiebreak is started by the player who was due to serve when the set was tied at 6–6. This player serves 1 point, which is then followed by the opponent player serving 2 points. After that, both players serve alternately for 2 points for the remainder of the tiebreak.

Players must change ends of the court after every 6 points. For example, after the tiebreak score stands at 3–3, 4–2, 6–6, and so on. This is done to incorporate the element of fairness in the tiebreak, keeping in mind the sun, wind, and other court conditions, which are then equal for both players.

VARIATIONS IN TIEBREAK RULES

Tiebreaks are integral to modern tennis as closely contested sets are now decided in a fair, decisive, and timely manner. Although tiebreaks have become a common feature in modern tennis, their rules have slight variations, depending on different countries and governing bodies of various tournaments.

James Van Alen introduced two types of tiebreakers in modern tennis in 1965. The first one ended after a maximum of 9 points was reached and was known as the 'sudden-death' tiebreaker. The second tiebreaker was called the 'lingering death' tiebreak and had a total of 12 points. While the first version of Alen's tiebreak is obsolete now, the second tiebreak is still applicable in tennis. The player or team that reaches a minimum of 7 points with a margin of at least 2 points wins the tiebreak and the set.

The US Open was the first Grand Slam to implement the tiebreak in 1970. However, it was incorporated for all sets, with the exception of the final set. The other Grand Slams followed, with the Australian Open in 1971, the French Open in 1973, and Wimbledon in 1979. All of them implemented the tiebreak for all sets that led to the final set. In 1989, the Davis Cup first adopted it in their scheme of things for all sets, except the final one. The rules were amended in 2016, when the tiebreaker was adopted for all sets.

In 2019, all the Grand Slams mutually agreed to implement final set tiebreaks. But the US Open uses a first-to-10 point tiebreak, which is a standard tiebreak when the game is tied at 6–6, whereas Wimbledon and the Australian Open use the traditional 12–12 tiebreak in the final set. Beginning from the 2022 French Open, all the Grand Slams agreed to a notable rule change in tennis. This was followed by the Olympic Games from 2024. This rule change was that a 10-point tiebreak would now be played out instead of 7-point tiebreak after the final deciding set was tied at 6 games each.

TIEBREAK STRATEGY

Every tennis player must have their tiebreak strategy in place to win sets and matches that are closely contested. Playing a tiebreak is a high-pressure situation where mental toughness, precision, strategic planning, and shot selection are so important to emerge as the winner. Studying the opponent's strengths and weaknesses in terms of a tiebreak is also crucial before the match, and that's where technology plays a major role.

The key things to focus on during a tiebreak are to remain calm under pressure, balance consistency with aggression, and not to commit any unforced errors. Winning a tiebreak, especially in the early stages of a tennis match, is a huge psychological boost because you have emerged triumphant in a close contest, and this can swing the momentum of the match in your favour.

At the Men's Futures tournament qualifications at Plantation, Florida, held in January 2013, Benjamin Balleret beat Guillaume Couillard in a staggering 70-point tiebreak 7–6, 6–1. The match was played without any chair umpire or linesmen, but the score has been verified by both the ITF and the ATP.

THE FOURTH KEY ERA IN TENNIS HISTORY

The Open Era is the fourth key area in tennis history. It began in 1968 when all the major tennis tournaments allowed professional tennis players to compete with amateurs, thus democratizing the sport and creating the global spectacle that we all love today. The first Grand Slam tournament to go open was the French Open.

2

TENNIS: RULES, BASICS, TERMS, AND CONCEPTS

Tennis is a racket sport that can be played among two individual players (Singles) or between two teams comprising two players each (Doubles). The playing area is a rectangular tennis court with fixed boundaries as per tennis laws. A net separates the two sides of the court. The game is all about getting a tennis ball to the other side of the court over the net by using a tennis racket. The ball has to fall within the boundaries of the court. When the player fails to get the ball over the net or keep it within the court boundaries, the opponent player gains a point.

Tennis has become a global spectator sport that is not only played by professional tennis players, but is also played as a recreational activity and fitness exercise by many fans.

VARIANTS OF TENNIS

Singles

A Singles game is played by only two players, one on each side of the court. When a player serves the ball to their opponent, they must begin play from the right half of the court by serving diagonally to the opponent player. Men have to play a best of five sets while women play a best of three sets. If a man wins three sets in a row or a woman wins two sets in a row, they win the match.

Doubles

A Doubles game features two players on each team. The partners in each team have to decide which of them will serve first, and their opponents must decide which one of them will receive the serve first. This serving and receiving role must change alternately for each game. When two gentlemen pair up to play Doubles, it is called men's Doubles. When two ladies play as a team, it is known as women's Doubles. When a gentleman and a lady team up as partners on both ends, the game is known as Mixed Doubles. So, Doubles in tennis has three subvariants. Both women's Doubles and Mixed Doubles have three sets per match.

THE PLAYING SURFACE

The playing surface area in tennis is derived from its earlier name 'lawn tennis', although the term 'tennis' is used more commonly today. The court surface was earlier composed of either grass or clay. As time went by, the playing surface also witnessed changes, along with the conditions of play. Sometimes, the surface also had to be changed to avoid inclement weather or other climatic disturbances that interrupted the game.

Wimbledon is played on a grass court, while the French Open features clay court surfaces. On the other hand, the US Open and Australian Open are played on hard courts. The Rolex Paris Masters is a tournament in France where players play on a carpet surface, which is also a removable court.

Major Tennis Tournaments Across the World

Name of Tournament	Venue (Country)
Wimbledon	England
US Open	USA
French Open (Roland Garros)	France
Australian Open	Australia
ATP World Tour	England
Rolex Shanghai Masters	China
Miami Open	USA
Rolex Paris Masters	France
Monte-Carlo Masters	Monaco
ATP World Tour Finals	Various European Countries

Professional tennis courts are of three primary types – grass, clay, and hard courts. Each surface offers a playing experience dissimilar to the others, mainly because of the variations of the speed and bounce of the tennis ball.

Artificial grass courts also exist, and these give a softer playing experience than what a real grass court offers.

Grass Courts	Clay Courts	Hard Courts
This is the fastest court, which is characterized by fast, low, and skidding bounces. Because matches on these courts are faster, a player with a good serve and volley game, like Roger Federer, dominates on these courts.	Clay courts have the slowest surfaces, which make them the most challenging surface to play on because they are physically draining. The surface causes the ball to have a higher bounce, and longer rallies are played out between the players as a result. A player with good defensive skills, playing from the baseline and armed with a good topspin, forehand, and backhand, like Rafael Nadal, dominates on clay.	Hard courts are the most versatile of all the three surfaces. They offer a consistent speed and moderate bounce of the tennis ball. Aggressive players like Novak Djokovic rule on such surfaces.

COURT DIMENSIONS

In its early days, tennis was played on courts shaped like an hourglass, with a net that was 4 feet 8 inches high. Since 1875, rectangular courts have been in use and were first introduced at Wimbledon in 1875. A modern-day net is 3 feet in the middle and 3.5 feet at the posts.

According to tennis law, all tennis courts should be rectangular in shape. The breadth of the court may vary sometimes because tennis is played in different variants or formats like Singles and Doubles. However, the length of the court remains unchanged. The standard tennis court is 27 feet wide and 78 feet long for Singles matches. The length is the same for Doubles, but the width changes to 36 feet to accommodate four players on the court instead of two.

The tennis court is divided into two equal halves, with the help of a net that must have a height of 0.914 metres from the ground. This net has to be tied parallel to the width of the court. A metal cable secures the net tightly and is attached to two net posts on either end. Because these two posts are always fixed, the tennis courts for both Singles and Doubles are not the same.

There are two lines drawn on the tennis courts to determine if the ball is in play or has gone outside the court while a tennis match is in progress. The lines on the wider ends of the court are called baselines, and the ones on the sides of the court are called sidelines. There is a baseline on each end of the court where the player serves from, and there are two sidelines at the sides on the court running parallel to each other, 1.37 metres apart. The first sideline is called the single sideline, and the parallel one is known as the Doubles sideline. On each side of the court, the area lying between the net and the service line, known as the service courts, is divided into equal parts by the centre service line. This centre service line is drawn parallel to the Singles sidelines and lies halfway between them. The service lines are 21 feet on each side of the net. All the court measurements are made to the outside of the lines, and it is mandatory that all the lines of the court are of the same colour. This colour must also contrast with the colour of the playing surface. Also, a total area of at least 120 feet in length and 60 feet in width must be provided for a proper tennis court. This is because more clear space is needed around the tennis court for the players to run and reach the balls. Two lines called service lines are drawn parallel to the net from the Singles sideline. These are 6.40 metres from the net on either side. The area that lies between the net and the service line is further divided into two equal halves with another line that is called the centre line, which runs perpendicular to the net and service line. As a standard rule, all the lines around the tennis court must be between 2.5 and 5 centimetres, with the sole exception of the baseline, which is almost 10 centimetres wide.

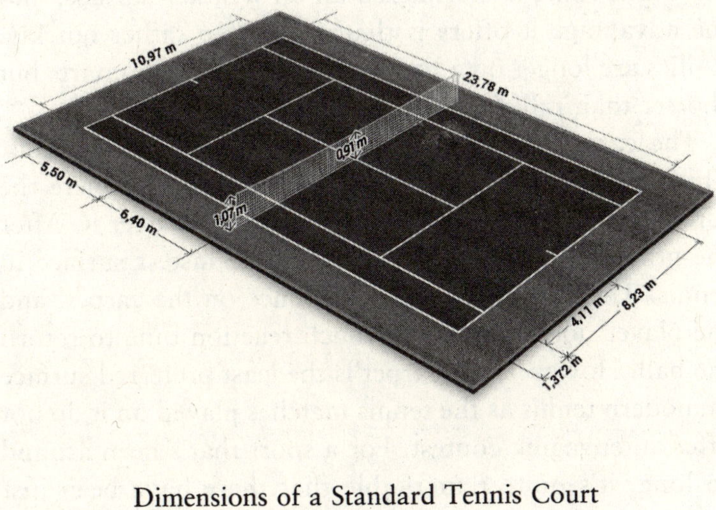

Dimensions of a Standard Tennis Court

TYPES OF COURT SURFACES

There are basically four types of court surfaces on which professional tennis is played today, including grass, clay, hard court, and carpet. The first three surfaces have been explained in the table on page 31.

Taling a little more about the most commonly used tennis courts today, hard courts were used in official tennis tournaments from the 1940s. This surface is made from concrete or asphalt, which has a coating of paint on top. Some sand is mixed with the paint to control the speed of the ball on the surface, and this, in turn, is dependent on the size and quantity of sand that is mixed with the paint. To cite an example, the two most popular hard court tennis tournaments use different materials in their hard courts. The US Open uses an acrylic hard court, while the Australian Open uses a synthetic hard court. The hard court is considered an all-weather surface, and the advantage it offers is that it dries up rather quickly. Rallies are longer on a hard court than on grass courts but shorter than rallies on clay courts.

The carpet is the fourth court surface used in tennis. This is, however, a removable court covering, where the turf makes up the surface, with sand spread over it. After the grass court, the carpet court is the fastest surface in tennis. There is not too much bounce on the carpet, and the player does not get too much reaction time to return the ball. However, the carpet is the least preferred surface in modern tennis as the tennis matches played on it do not offer an engaging contest. For a sport that's been around so long, it's quite remarkable that there have been just two major rules changes in tennis since the 19th century. Since the 1890s, the rules have been mostly constant. The server had to keep one foot on the ground at all times until 1961. The second was the adoption of the tiebreak in tennis in the 1970s. Innovations like the Hawk-Eye, a point-challenge system where electronic review equipment is used, have made the game more scientific and decisions more accurate.

INTERESTING TENNIS LAWS

If an additional ball happens to enter the court while a tennis match is on, the point has to be replayed.

If a player catches a ball before it bounces during play, the point is given to the opponent. This is regardless of where the ball is positioned. Even if it is outside, but in the air, it must hit the ground first to be ruled out.

The player or team receiving the service can stand anywhere in the court, except the service box.

In Doubles, if the team communicates loudly when a game is in progress, the point is given to the opponent team.

If the player who is serving swings at the ball, he/she has tossed up in the air and misses, it is deemed as a fault.

TENNIS EQUIPMENT

Essential player equipment for tennis includes rackets, tennis balls, tennis shoes, and a dress code, which may include additional accessories like wristbands and headbands. Wristbands are worn around the wrists to stop the sweat from the body of the player from wetting their palms or the racket to allow convenience at play. Headbands are used to absorb the sweat and keep away a player's hair from their face, especially if they have long hair. A cap can also work as a substitute for the headband. Running shoes do not suffice for playing tennis as they do not provide the lateral support a tennis player needs. Tennis shoes must be worn as they give a player more stability and help them to move sideways better and not slide away while chasing the ball on court. The attire should be light material made out of polyester that doesn't absorb sweat to keep the player cool. Male tennis players must wear shorts that don't cover the knees for better movement.

TENNIS TERMS IN ALPHABETICAL ORDER

Ace: If the serve cannot be touched by the receiver and the ball flies past them, it is termed an ace.

Advantage: The next point that a player wins after deuce is called the advantage point. It is equal to game point as the player wins the game if they win the next point. But if the opponent wins the next point instead, the score in the game is back to deuce.

Advantage Set: An advantage set is the final set of a tennis match where a player or team must win at least 6 games and win the set with a 2-game lead. An advantage set is different from a tiebreak set because they don't end with a tiebreak when the score becomes 6–6 in a set. Play in the set continues until a player or a team manages to get that 2-game advantage to win the final set and the match.

Alley: The area of the court that lies between the sidelines of Singles and Doubles is called the alley.

Break: In tennis, a break is when a player wins a game when the opponent is serving, thus breaking serve. A break is a key moment in a game as it often tilts the set in favour of the player who has broken the opponent's service. Breaking serve twice in a set is called a double break.

Break Back: When a player breaks serve in the very next game after his service has been broken, it is called a break back in tennis.

Break Point: The last point of a particular game that is about to be won by the opponent as the other player serves is called the break point. This is because the opponent breaks the other player's serve and wins the game. The player who is serving can win the point and save the break point as well.

Ball in Play: If a player hits a fixed structure like a net post during a rally, and the ball rebounds to bounce back into the opponent's court, it is considered to be ball in play, and the point holds good. However, if the ball bounces back to the same side of the court, the point is awarded to the opponent.

Backhand Smash: When a player uses their backhand to smash the ball, it's called a backhand smash.

Backcourt: It is the area that lies between the baseline and the service line on the tennis court.

Backspin: It is a tennis shot that rotates the ball backwards after it is hit with the racket. The backspin is also called the slice or underspin in tennis parlance.

Backswing: When a tennis player swings the racket backwards to prepare to hit the ball in a forward motion, it is called the backswing.

Bagel: Bagel is the American English term for winning or losing a set 6–0. The shape of the zero has been equated to the shape of a bagel, which is round.

Breadstick: Breadstick is the American English term for winning or losing a set with a score of 6–1. Here, the straight shape of a breadstick has been compared to the straight shape of 1.

Backboard: This is a vertical wall, usually with the image of a tennis net painted on it. The backboard is used to practise by a solitary tennis player so that the ball bounces back and they can practise without a tennis partner.

Ball Toss: It is the motion of throwing the ball up in the air just before the serve.

Ball Machine: This machine discharges tennis balls to the tennis player at speeds equal to those of a human. The ball machine allows a tennis player to practise their strokes without the need for a human partner.

Ball Boy/Ball Girl: Children are given the task of fetching the tennis balls that have gone out of play from the tennis court. These kids are called ball boys/girls. They also supply the balls to the players when they are ready to serve. There are two positions that are employed by the ball boys/girls. The first is the net position, where they kneel close to the net in full alert mode to run across the court and collect the ball when it goes out of play. The second is the back position, where they stand quietly at the back of the court where the arena ends. Ball boys/girls standing here are responsible for giving the balls to be selected to the tennis player who is about to serve.

Banana Shot/Banana Forehand: The banana shot is a forehand shot hit down the line by a player with enough spin to curve in the air outside and then fall back into the court again. This was Spanish legend Rafael Nadal's signature shot.

Baseline: The baseline is the line at the furthest ends of the court and denotes the boundary of the tennis court, which is the play area. The opponent gains the point if the ball travels over the baseline.

Baseliner: The tennis player who plays his game from the baseline instead of approaching the net is a baseliner or baseline player. This is normally on the slower clay surfaces, where this type of player is heavily reliant on the power of his ground strokes.

Block: A block or a blocked shot or a blocked return is a defensive shot that has very little backswing. It has a shortened action instead of a full swing and is usually engaged in while returning a powerful serve.

Backhand: The backhand is a shot played by a tennis player with the arms holding the racket across the body. In the backhand, the back of the hand faces the direction of the shot, opposite of a forehand.

Boxed Set: When a player wins a career slam in Singles, Doubles, and Mixed Doubles, it is called a boxed set. This means that the tennis player has won at least one title in each of these tennis variants at all four of the Grand Slam venues. The boxed set has been achieved just four times in tennis history, and all the winners have been women. The lucky winners are Doris Hart, Margaret Court (twice), and Martina Navratilova.

Chair Umpire and Line Umpires: A professional tennis match has a chair umpire, who is the chief official and the final authority on the court. The chair umpire sits in a high chair and conducts the coin toss, calls out the score, manages the players, and ensures that the match is played according to the rules. The line umpires or line judges are responsible for calling if a ball is in or out of the lines. Line umpires or judges need good eyesight, great powers of concentration, and must be good team players. A chair judge has the power to overrule the call of a line judge if they think that the call was incorrect. However, thanks to the advent of technology, line calls and disputes have become much easier to resolve.

Can Opener: This is a type of serve that is dished up by a right-handed tennis player. The can opener is a serve with a slice that curves away sharply from the player receiving the serve.

Cannon Ball: A cannonball is a type of serve that is very fast and flat.

Career Grand Slam: Tennis players, who have won all four Grand Slam titles at least once in their playing career, and not necessarily in the same calendar year, have achieved a Career Grand Slam.

Career Golden Slam: A tennis player who has won the gold medal in the Olympics, apart from winning a Career Grand Slam, has achieved the title of a Career Golden Slam. In Singles, only five players have achieved this feat in tennis history. They are Steffi Graf, Andre Agassi, Rafael Nadal, Serena Williams, and Novak Djokovic.

Centre Mark: It is a small mark at the centre of the baseline. The player must stand on the right side of the mark according to the score.

Carve: This is a groundstroke shot that utilizes both sidespin and underspin.

Challenge: When a player challenges the line umpire's decision and asks for an official review of where the ball landed using electronic ball tracking technology, it is known as a challenge in tennis.

Change-over: This refers to the change of ends when tennis players rest for 90 seconds before changing ends on the court after every odd-numbered game.

Chip: A chip is blocking a shot with underspin to create a low trajectory.

Chip and Charge: This is an approach shot where the player hits a slice shot and then quickly runs or charges forward towards the net to try and put the opponent under pressure as they return the shot.

Chop: This shot is the opposite of the topspin and is executed with extreme underspin.

Closed Stance: The closed stance is a classic posture in tennis in which the tennis player hits the ball as their body is at an angle that is parallel to the baseline while their back is turned to the opponent.

Code Violation: This is basically the violation of a rule in a professional tennis match in which the chair umpire identifies and calls out the violation by the tennis player. The first violation is a warning. The second code violation results in a point penalty, while the third and further violations result in a game penalty for each violation. Sometimes, a code violation may be severe enough for the chair umpire to ban the player from taking further part in the match instantly, without the three stages of violation. A monetary fine may also follow each violation by the tennis player, which leads to a deduction of his match fees.

Consolidate: To consolidate means to hold serve in the next game after the serve is broken in the previous one.

Cross Over: When a player crosses the net and enters the opponent's court it is called a cross over. This can be done in a friendly fashion after the end of a match. But if this is done otherwise, like protesting a decision like a line call and arguing with the umpire or confronting the opponent, for example, it leads to a code violation.

Crosscourt Shot: A crosscourt shot is when a player hits the ball diagonally into the court of the opponent.

Deuce: If both players reach scores of 40, it is known as deuce. In the French Open, deuce is known as 'egalite', which means 'equal'.

Double Fault: A double fault happens in tennis when the player who is serving fails to get both his first serve and second serve right. The ball either hits the net or does not land in the correct service box of the opponent. If a double fault happens with two consecutive service faults, the point is given to the opponent player/players.

Dead Ball: A dead ball is an old ball that has lost its bounce and, therefore, cannot be used in play. These balls emit a hollow sound when hit with the racket.

Dead Rubber: In a competition like the Fed Cup (now known as the Billie Jean King Cup) or the Davis Cup, if a match is played just for the formality of completing the fixture as the winner of the tie has already been decided, that particular match is called a dead rubber. This is because the outcome or result of the match has no bearing whatsoever on the competition. Sometimes, lower-ranked players play the dead rubber to gain some big-match experience.

Deep Shot: A shot that lands very close to the baseline is called a deep shot as it would have gone out if it was only a bit longer.

Default: Default is the disqualification of a player in a tennis match after the player has received four code violation warnings from the chair umpire, normally for bad conduct on court, like showing dissent, abusive language, smashing rackets, etc. A double default takes place when both players participating in the Singles match are disqualified from the game. A player also faces a default if they miss a match without a valid reason.

Deuce Court: The deuce court refers to the right side of the court of a tennis player. It has been named thus because it is the area where the ball is served when the score is deuce or 40–40.

Dig: A shot where the player manages to hit the ball just before it bounces twice is called the dig. The name is on account of the racket position, which is downward and similar to a shovel digging a hole.

Double Break Point: When the player has the advantage of two breaks of service in a set as his opponent is serving, it is called a double break point. This is when the opponent is down 15–40.

Double-Handed Forehand: When the forehand shot is made by a player using both hands, it is called a double-handed forehand.

Double-Handed Backhand: When the backhand shot is made by a player using both hands, it is called a double-handed backhand.

Down the Line: When a player returns the ball straight along the sideline on the opponent's court, usually making it impossible to play the shot, it is known as a down-the-line forehand or backhand, depending on how the ball is hit.

Drive: It is a groundstroke that is hit with a flat trajectory.

Drive Volley: A drive volley, or a swing volley, is made by a player with a full swing of the racket or a topspin drive. It is a similar shot to the forehand or backhand swing but is made from shoulder height at a fast pace.

Drop Shot: A drop shot is when a player hits the ball so lightly, normally with backspin, that it just goes over the net to land near the net on the opponent's side of the court. The idea is to catch the opponent off guard, who is standing away from the net, expecting a faster return.

Drop Volley: When a player makes a drop shot from a position from which a volley can be made, it is called a drop volley.

Drop a Set: To lose a set in a match is also called dropping a set.

Elbow: It is the corner of the baseline and the Doubles alley.

Fault: When a player fails to serve the ball in the service box of the opponent because of a service error, it is called a fault.

Foot Fault: A foot fault happens when a player steps on the baseline or over it while they are serving the ball to the opponent. It may also happen if the player steps on or across the centre hash mark.

Flat: A flat or flat shot is one that has very little spin and is normally hit hard.

Flatliner: A flatliner is someone who hits the ball flat with a low trajectory. The ball is shot with great depth and accuracy, which makes it difficult for a return or results in a weak return by the opponent. Examples of a flatliner include Andre Agassi in men's tennis and Lindsay Davenport in women's tennis.

Follow-through: A follow-through is when the swing of the racket continues after the ball has been hit by a player. The follow-through is important to build power, control, and consistency in a player's shots and overall game. It also helps in better shot placement and protects a player against injuries.

Forced Error: When a player commits an error because of the good play of the opponent, it is known as a forced error, as the opponent's better play has forced the error out of the player. But if the player makes a mistake and concedes the point to the opponent because of that, it is called an unforced error.

Frame Shot: When the ball hits the frame of the racket rather than the strings because of a mishit, it is known as a frame shot.

Forehand: The forehand is a shot played by a tennis player with the racket when their palm is facing in the direction of the shot.

First and Second Serve: If a player doesn't get his first serve right by making it land within the correct service box of the opponent, they are allowed a second serve to get the ball over the net into the opponent's court. This next attempt to serve is called the second serve. The number of times a player gets his first serve correct is analysed in percentage with the help of technology. This is called the player's first serve percentage.

Game Point: The last point of a particular game is called game point.

Game Set and Match: This expression is used to conclude a match to indicate that one of the tennis players has emerged as the winner of the match.

Golden Set: When a player wins a set without conceding a single point, it is called a golden set.

Grip: A grip is how a tennis player holds his racket when he plays his shots during the course of play. Players might change their grips during a match, depending on the shots that they want to hit. The most commonly used grips are the Continental, the Eastern, and the Western grips.

Groundstroke: A groundstroke is a forehand or backhand shot played by a player after the ball bounces once on the court.

Half Court: The area of the court near the service line is called half court.

Half Volley: A half volley is a groundstroke shot played immediately after the ball has bounced on court or just as the ball has bounced, with the racket placed close to the ground.

Hawk-eye: This is a computer system that tracks the path of the tennis ball during replay to determine if the ball has landed inside or outside the court. This computer system is connected to multiple cameras, and the Hawk-Eye is normally employed when the player challenges the umpire's call.

Hitting Partner or Sparring Partner: A professional tennis player normally engages a specialist called a hitting partner or sparring partner to practise their strokes while training for a tennis tournament.

Hold Serve: When a player wins the game while serving, it is called holding one's serve.

I-formation: This formation is used in Doubles when the non-serving member of the team crouches at the centre service line as his partner serves to meet the crosscourt return that will come from the opponent team.

Inside-in: This is when a player runs around the backhand side to hit a down-the-line forehand. The reverse holds good for a down-the-line backhand.

Inside-out: When a player runs around the backhand side and hits a crosscourt forehand, it is known as an inside-out tennis shot. The reverse holds good for an inside-out backhand.

IPIN: IPIN stands for International Player Identification Number. This is a registration number that is needed for all professional tennis players and is operated by the International Tennis Federation, the governing body of tennis.

Jamming: When a tennis player serves or hits a return that is directed straight into the opponent's body, it is called jamming.

Kick Serve: This is a spin serve that falls and bounces high. That's how it got its name. The kick serve is also called the American twist because it originated in the USA in the late 1880s.

Knock-up: A knock-up is a practice or warm-up session that normally takes place before the start of a tennis match.

Kenin-hold: This term is used to describe when a player serves to win the game from being down 0–40. The player holds their serve by taking 4 consecutive points to win the game. The Kenin-Hold has been named after American tennis player Sofia Kenin. In the finals of the 2020 Australian Open, Kenin was down 0–40 in the final against Garbiñe Muguruza. But she held her serve to win the game, match, and the Australian Open title.

Let: An umpire makes a 'let' call (many think he is calling 'net') to replay a point in one of the following cases:

- When the ball touches the net after a serve but lands in the service box, it's called a 'service let'. This is when the serve needs to be made again and why many think the umpire is calling 'net' instead of 'let'.
- When there is an interruption in play because of a dispute in a line call or another ball entering the court

from another tennis court, an 'in-game let' is called by the umpire, and the server has to serve again.

- When an umpire calls a 'let', it does not change the score. Instead, the point is simply replayed from the beginning, like the same serve or from where the interruption took place.

The origin of the term 'let' is from an older meaning of the same word, which means to obstruct or hinder.

Let-check: The let-check is an electronic sensor on the net that helps a chair umpire to call lets thanks to the vibration being detected.

Lingering Death Tiebreak: The lingering death tiebreak is a version of the tiebreak that is played as the best of 12 points. A 2-point advantage is needed in the tiebreak to win the set.

Lob: The lob is a tennis stroke where the ball is hit high above the net with the intention of placing the ball above the head of the opponent and out of his reach, behind him.

Long: Long is a call by the line judges to denote that the ball has landed outside the court, beyond the baseline.

Love: 'Love all' is announced at a score of 0–0 in tennis when the game begins. The first point, 15–0, is spoken as 'fifteen love', the second as 'thirty love', and so on.

Love Game and Love Hold: 'To hold to love' means winning the game while the opponent fails to score a single point in the game. The game is known as a love game.

Match Point: It is the last point of the match when a player is about to win against his opponent. The opponent can win the point and save the match point.

Mac-cam: This is a high-speed slow-motion video camera that shows instant replays of close shots that land on or near the baseline that become controversial calls. The MAC in the name has been inspired by American tennis player John McEnroe, who was notorious for his passionate disputes with the chair umpire over close line calls. Thanks to the Mac-Cam, the perfect visual aid is provided for umpires. How McEnroe must be wishing that he had it in his time!

New Balls: New balls refer to a new set of balls that replace the old ones after 7 or 9 games in the match have been played. One must remember here that the knock-up or practice before the match is equivalent to 2 games. They are provided after the chair umpire says, 'New balls, please.' Having new balls in due course is essential as the repeated strokes with the racket makes the tennis balls heat up and lose their velocity and pressure. This leads to a loss of bounce as well. According to tennis courtesy, a player serving with the new ball shows it to the opponent before doing so.

No-man's Land: This is the area between the baseline and the service line. This zone is where players are most vulnerable, as they are not close to the net to volley properly, and they are too close to play ground strokes effectively.

Overhead: The overhead is a stroke hit by a player over their head. It is called a smash if it is hit very strongly. However, all smashes are called overheads, but not every overhead shot is a smash.

Overrule: When the chair umpire reverses a call made by the line judge, it is known as an overrule.

Percentage Tennis: It's a tennis strategy that is reliant on calculated decisions instead of making high-risk, low-percentage shots. The focus is on winning by playing to one's strengths and making smart choices consistently. The strategy involves keeping the ball in play while waiting for the opponent to make an error.

Perfect Game: A perfect game is when the server hits four aces to win the game.

Point Penalty: When a point is awarded to the opponent because of successive code violations made by a player, it is called point penalty.

Rally: When the tennis players play shots continuously to each other to win a point in the game, it is called a rally in tennis. The players have to return the ball to the opponent's side by hitting it over the net and make sure it falls within the area of the sideline and baseline of the opponent's court.

Racket Abuse: When a player throws their racket to the ground or smashes it in anger or frustration, it's called racket abuse. This can lead to a warning from the umpire or a loss of points.

Rating Systems: Tennis players are rated according to their skills and match performances. The first global tennis rating system is the World Tennis Number (WTN), developed by the ITF, which rates players on a 40–1 scale. 40 is for beginners, while 1 is for the topmost professionals. The second rating system is the Universal Tennis Rating (UTR), which rates all players on a scale of 1.00–16.50.

Return Ace: When a player returns his opponent's serve in such a manner that the server is unable to touch the ball with his racket, it's called a return ace.

Set Point: The last point of a particular set is called the set point.

Serve: The tennis player standing behind the baseline tosses the ball high in the air and strikes it with his racket before it falls on the ground to make it travel over the net into the opponent's area. This is called a serve, and the players must stand diagonally on the court while they serve and receive the serve. Each serve starts from the right half of the court.

Scratch: A scratch is a situation when a player withdraws from a match because of an injury.

Seed: A player is seeded in a tournament according to their ranking so that the top-ranked players do not have to face other top-ranked players in the early rounds of the competition. The name draws inspiration from the seeds that are scattered over the ground so that they can be planted.

Shot Clock: A clock displayed to the public and used in between points to make sure that a tennis player serves in 25 seconds. The shot clock was first used in a Grand Slam at the 2018 Australian Open.

Spin: Spin in tennis is when the ball rotates with its movement in the air, which in turn affects its bounce and trajectory.

Stance: The stance of a player is the way they stand before they hit the tennis ball.

Sudden Death Tiebreak: Sudden death tiebreak is played as the best of 9 points, with the last point being the decider to win the set.

Super Tiebreak: This is a tiebreak with a first to 10 points format and is normally used in Doubles to decide a match instead of playing the third set. Super tiebreak is also known as champions tiebreak.

Sweetspot: It's the central part of the racket head, which is the best part to make contact with the ball for maximum control and power in a shot.

Tanking: Tanking refers to losing a match on purpose or intentionally losing a set that is not vital to focus on a set that decides the match. Nicky Kyrgios received a temporary ban when he tanked at the 2016/17 Shanghai Open.

Topspin: Topspin is when the top of the tennis ball rotates in the direction the ball is travelling. This makes the ball dip and bounce at a higher angle to the court.

Toss: The toss of a coin decides which player will serve first in the match.

Underarm Serve: A legal serve in tennis, the underarm serve is when the player serves from below the shoulder level.

Underspin: Also called the backspin or undercut, underspin is when the top of the ball rotates away from the direction the ball is travelling. This makes the ball float and bounce at a lower angle to the court.

Unseeded Player: A tennis player who is not seeded in a tournament is called an unseeded player.

Upset: When a top-ranked player is defeated by a lower-ranked player, it is called an upset.

Volley: A volley is an aggressive move in tennis when a player runs quickly towards the net during a rally to strike the ball on the full with their racket. A volley gives the player an edge to place the ball wherever they want on the opponent's court and gain a point. A volley is usually backed by a powerful serve, normally on a grass court where the surface is fast, and this style of play is called a 'serve and volley game'.

Walkover: A walkover is given to a tennis player who is adjudged the winner of a match that is not played because of their opponent's failure to start the match because of injury or any other reason.

Wildcard: A player is given a wildcard entry in a tennis tournament even if his rank is not suitable. This is usually when a tennis player pulls out of a tournament or a chance is given to local players or those making a comeback in tennis.

Yo-yo: When a player hits a backspin shot so that the ball lands on the opponent's court and then returns to the player's court after the first bounce, it's called a yo-yo.

3

THE GRAND SLAMS – I

WIMBLEDON

Wimbledon Logo

Twice upon a time in the valley of the tears
An auctioneer is bidding for a box of fading years
And the elephants are dancing on the graves of squealing mice.

Anyone for tennis, wouldn't that be nice?
And the ice creams are all melting on the streets of bloody beer
While the beggars stain the pavements with fluorescent Christmas cheer
And the Bentley-driving Guru is putting up his price.
Anyone for tennis, wouldn't that be nice?

(Eric Clapton and Martin Sharp, Cream)

Anyone for Tennis **Song by Cream**

British rock band Cream's iconic song 'Anyone for Tennis' serves as a fitting tribute to the sport and is also reflective of the general mood of the oldest tennis Grand Slam in the world – Wimbledon.

Not only is Wimbledon the oldest Grand Slam, but it is also considered the most prestigious tournament by tennis players and pundits. The Brits love to call it the world's leading tennis tournament. The French, Americans, and Australians might have something to say about that, though.

Speaking of the French, tennis player Jean Borota must love Wimbledon more than Roland-Garros itself. In 1924, Borota won his first Wimbledon championship and took to the tournament like a fish to water. Forty years later, the man was still competing in the main draw of the tournament. In 1977, Jean Borota played in the Wimbledon veteran's Doubles at the ripe young age of 78. *Sacré bleu* is the word!

However, some of the greatest tennis players, like Novak Djokovic, Carlos Alcaraz, and Angelique Kerber, to name a few, have confessed that they dreamt of holding up the Wimbledon trophy as kids. Imagine the feeling when they actually managed to do so!

The charm and hype surrounding Wimbledon is undeniable and unrivalled. It is the only Grand Slam that is still played on grass courts. It's interesting to note that both the US Open and the Australian Open were played on grass once upon a time, before they switched to the hard court format. Hanging on in quiet desperation is definitely the English way!

But to be fair, Wimbledon is actually the largest tennis tournament that is played on grass today. More than 5,00,000 fans congregate here every year in the months of June and July, when all the other popular sports like football and cricket take a back seat. In fact, some of the stars of cricket, football, and other sports are witnessed in the box as well, dressed in their resplendent best and rooting for their favourite tennis players. Tennis players from over 60 countries in the world compete to win top honours at Wimbledon. There are 13 different categories with fantastic trophies and attractive prize money on offer.

The suburb of Wimbledon is located 7 miles south-west of Charing Cross, and this suburb bursts into life and a flurry of activity when the tennis tournament is held.

WIMBLEDON: A BRIEF HISTORY

The name Wimbledon means 'Wynnman's Hill' (not to be confused with Henman Hill). The All England Lawn Tennis and Croquet Club is responsible for staging this tournament. Its first ground was situated off Worple Road, Wimbledon. The lawns at the ground were arranged such that the principal court was located in the middle, with the others arranged around it. That gave rise to the famous name 'Centre Court'.

Wimbledon has been hosted by the All England Club in the London suburb of Wimbledon since 1877. That's 70 years before India got her independence from British colonial rule! But before the tournament began, it was advertised as a 'lawn tennis meeting, open to all amateurs'. Even YOU could have participated in Wimbledon back then, when the Open Era had not begun. Sadly, you can't now!

The first Wimbledon match was held on 9 July 1877 at Worple Road in Wimbledon. The Gentlemen's Singles was the only event played then and was won by Spencer Gore. The final was attended by about 200 spectators, and tickets were priced at one shilling. 1877 also saw the introduction of the rectangular court by the Wimbledon tournament committee. Before this, tennis courts were shaped like an hourglass, where the narrowest part of the court was the net.

In 1884, additions were made by the All England Club, and Ladies' Singles and Gentlemen's Doubles became new attractions at Wimbledon. In 1913, Ladies' Doubles and Mixed Doubles were also added to complete the circle.

The famous white dress code of Wimbledon was introduced in 1963. However, the totally white dress code came into force only in 1995, although the majorly white dress code was implemented in 1963. 2014 saw an expansion of this fetish with white to cover player accessories as well.

From Wimbledon's inception in 1877, a challenge round system was in place till as long as 1921. Under this rule, the defending champion automatically qualified for the next year's final at Wimbledon and had to play against only one challenger, who beat everyone else to face him. Thankfully, the Brits decided to scrap this system in 1992, but it's perplexing why they took so long to do it. Thankfully, the defending champion now has to battle it out right from the first round. This democratic move probably gave rise to the term 'upset' in tennis, whenever a top seed loses to a lower-ranked player.

Since 1922, tennis has grown and evolved considerably, and so has Wimbledon. New courts have been built, and the 11,500-seat No. 1 Court is prominent among them. So are courts 18 and 19. But the major attraction is the famous 'Henman Hill', with its gigantic TV screen, which has become an iconic and modern Wimbledon attraction.

WIMBLEDON ATTRACTIONS

Wimbledon Village is a lovely cosmopolitan London suburb that is worthy of a visit any time of the year, not just when the tennis action is on. Wimbledon boasts of some of the best restaurants and fashion stores. Just down the hill in Wimbledon town, one can indulge in a gastronomical delight at the famous Italian restaurant, San Lorenzo. If you are not a big fan of Italian food, you can always spot your favourite tennis stars in this joint while you pretend to munch on a pizza or something. The Italian joint is frequented by celebrities and food lovers alike, so don't be zapped if you see Roger Federer order pasta and meatballs at the table next to you. The reason why Federer might be there even after retirement is that he simply loves Wimbledon. He certainly has good reason to, having won the tournament a record eight times. That's the most men's Singles titles in the Open Era of Wimbledon. He also loves Italian food, especially pasta and pizza. In fact, he loves Italian cuisine so much that he's also been featured in the Barilla pasta commercials. Roger that!

> Tennis icon Martina Navratilova also loves Wimbledon and Italian cuisine like pasta. She's won the Wimbledon women's Singles a record nine times in the Open Era. That's one more title than Roger Federer. Advantage Navratilova!

The original medieval High Street at Wimbledon includes the St. Mary's Church and the Old Rectory. It links the wide open spaces of Wimbledon Common with Wimbledon Hill. One can also visit a range of top-quality shops, pubs, restaurants, wine bars, pavement cafés, boutiques, and businesses here to make your stay pleasant and memorable.

For designer wear shopping, head to Matches, which stocks all the big international designers. The New Wimbledon Theatre offers diverse and exciting productions. The Wimbledon Lawn Tennis Museum is highly recommended for tennis fans. Explore the history of Wimbledon, see the celebrated trophies, and take a grand tour of the legendary Centre Court. While you're at it, do watch some tennis as well!

FAMOUS WIMBLEDON TRADITIONS

Strawberries and Cream

George Peele, a notable playwright who was a contemporary of William Shakespeare, wrote a song in his play *The Old Wives' Tale* that compared strawberries with summer and delight. It goes like this:

> *When as the rye reach to the chin,*
> *And chopcherry, chopcherry, ripe within,*
> *Strawberries swimming in the cream,*
> *And schoolboys playing in the stream...*

Although poet and dramatist George Peele is famously remembered for his supposed collaboration with Shakespeare on the play *Titus Andronicus*, this song is reflective of the British obsession with strawberries, which continues to date. How else would you explain the fact that an astonishing amount of about 28,000 kilos of strawberries are consumed during Wimbledon, served with 10,000 litres of cream every year? That is what is claimed by Wimbledon's official website. That roughly translates to 1.6 million individual strawberries. If you were to lay all those strawberries in a straight line, they'd almost cover 37 miles end to end! Imagine that.

That's not all. All of those strawberries are sourced from just one farm in Kent called Hugh Lowe Farms, a family-owned business. They have been the sole supplier of strawberries to Wimbledon for almost 30 years, supplying the specific variety called the Malling Centenary. Before dawn every morning, two teams of 40 pickers land on this farm to pick more than 1,00,000 strawberries for one day's consumption. The first of those millions of strawberries was served in 1953 without cream. This only happened after the queen issued a decree that anyone who didn't buy any strawberries when they were watching tennis would lose their kneecaps. The queen must have really loved her strawberries. But the Brits took their queen seriously and went on a wild strawberry ride, which has become a tradition today. In 1970, cream was added to the traditional fare due to health concerns raised that the consumption of strawberries on their own might cause heart and weight problems. This was as serious as losing kneecaps, and cream was the solution. Thankfully, one can skip the strawberries today and watch the tennis without any danger of losing their kneecaps. Strangely, the consumption of strawberries has only increased. Maybe it's the cream! Whatever it is, there's no denying that strawberries and cream are as important in Wimbledon as a tennis racket.

GRASS

N.B: *Grass here refers to the playing surface of Wimbledon and is not to be confused with anything else.*

Wimbledon is the only major tournament that is still played on grass, which has become a tradition here, as all the other Grand Slams have switched to other surfaces. Grass is probably the chosen surface at Wimbledon because it is abundant in England. It also brings about a unique style of play that is pleasant to watch.

The grass court has the fastest surface among all the courts commonly used in tennis. The surface tends to favour tennis players like Roger Federer and Martina Navratilova, who have a good serve and volley game. That explains why the two have the most Wimbledon titles in the Open Era among men and women, respectively. The reason the serve becomes crucial on a grass court is that the ball bounces lower on grass than on a hard court or clay surface. There are no long rallies as a result, and the points are usually short. Other prominent tournaments that are played on grass include the Stuttgart Open and Halle Open in Germany.

A rest day is scheduled at Wimbledon in the middle of the tournament. This is to allow the grass to recover from the heavy pounding! During this break, the ground staff waters the grass meticulously and makes it match-ready for the next round of matches in the second week at Wimbledon. Four weeks before Wimbledon is scheduled to commence, the grass is carefully cut down to precisely 8 mm in height, which has been deduced to be the optimum height for playing tennis. Every day, while the tournament is in progress, the ground staff ensures that the lawn is mowed to keep the grass height at 8 mm and repaints the lines religiously. Such dedication would have made Sherlock Holmes proud. There is little respite for the ground staff even after the tournament ends. After just a week, preparations begin for next year's grass at Wimbledon.

THE WEATHER

Wimbledon takes place during the English summer. But if you thought that the event is blessed by sunshine and clear blue skies, think again. There is a famous saying that without inclement weather, Wimbledon would be as popular as baseball in Europe. Rain has become a part of the Wimbledon tradition. So much so that they had an old Sir Cliff Richard singing his old chartbusters to entertain the crowd at Wimbledon whenever it rained. It probably inspired Sir Cliff to come up with his song 'Summer Rain' in 1981 as well.

Thankfully, there are no stoppages in play these days, thanks to technology. A retractable roof has been installed, which has killed the tradition of live songs during inclement weather. No more 'rain stops play' at Wimbledon. No more Cliff Richard, too!

HENMANIA

The British are understandably proud of a tournament like Wimbledon. But it was a matter of national agony when no British player managed to win the Singles event at Wimbledon for a long time since 1936, when Fred Perry

> The temperature of a tennis ball impacts its bounce. The Wimbledon tennis balls are kept at a temperature of 68°F. The gas molecules inside the ball expand with the rise in temperature, making the ball bounce higher during play. The molecules shrink when exposed to lower temperatures, making the ball bounce lower. Every year, Wimbledon uses more than 50,000 tennis balls so that the best balls are served up to play with.

achieved the feat. Virginia Wade was the last British woman to win the women's Singles title in 1977.

Finally, Scottish player Andy Murray managed to end 77 years of British heartbreak. Murray won Wimbledon in 2013 and repeated the success three years later, in 2016. There was a lot of hype before Murray won as Tim Henman was expected to break the jinx by winning Wimbledon. Confident of his success, the Brits even dedicated a hill to his name. But Timmy flattered to deceive. He failed to even reach the finals of Wimbledon, although he reached the semi-finals as many as four times in 1998, 1999, 2001, and 2002. 2001 was the closest Henman came to reaching the final, when he lost a close five-set match to eventual winner Goran Ivanišević. But Henman was a fine tennis player who kept British hopes alive, even though he could never win a Grand Slam. He also reached the semi-finals of both the French Open and the US Open in 2004. Tragically, Henman Hill, which was unofficially named after him, is now commonly referred to as Mount Murray, Murray Mountain, and Murrayfield to honour Andy Murray's Wimbledon triumphs. Such is life!

Thankfully, the BBC and other media outlets still call it Henman Hill, probably because it sounds better. Henman Hill or Murray Mountain is basically an area of grass that stands proudly at the northern end of the grounds. A giant television screen broadcasts important matches before a huge crowd.

BBGs

BBGs, or ball boys and girls, play an important role in the smooth functioning of the tournament and are a traditional part of Wimbledon. Each year, 250 young kids are selected from 27 schools nearby to serve as ball boys and girls at Wimbledon. Their average age is 15.

Ball Boys and Girls at Wimbledon 2025

Being a ball boy/girl at Wimbledon is serious business as the tournament sets rather high standards for everyone. It's not easy to keep track of the fast-paced tennis ball when someone like Jannik Sinner is serving at 135 miles per hour. They have to take a test before being selected to ensure that they can stand still for at least three minutes. Yes, that's difficult for Gen Z these days. The ones who can, have to attend weekly training sessions, and this training is almost a military-like regime. One needs to train eight hours a week for four months before the tournament begins.

UNIFORMS

Dark green and purple are the traditional colours of Wimbledon. Tennis players must wear white, but a hint of colour is allowed. The chair umpire, linesmen, and ball boys and girls were clad in green clothing till 2005. But the 2006 Wimbledon Championships saw a change, as they were seen in new navy blue and cream uniforms from famed American designer Ralph Lauren.

Wimbledon has a strict dress code. Any coloured trim that the players sport on their all-white clothing must be less than 1 cm in width. The dress code is applicable to socks, shoes, and even undergarments, and players have been fined for not following the rules.

In a rule that might seem baffling to many in these modern times, tennis players who participate in the Wimbledon Championships are required to submit their clothing to the All England Lawn Tennis and Croquet Club for approval before the start of the tournament. The seal of approval is not just restricted to clothing, but also to accessories like caps, shoes, and wristbands. The all-white dress code of the AELTC must be strictly adhered to, and samples of clothing have to be submitted at least 90 days in advance for them to be reviewed. That's only fair, as there are too many players, and hence, too many clothes and accessories.

The first women who played at Wimbledon wore full-length dresses, which must have been pretty cumbersome during rallies, surely. The men had to play in full-length pants until 1946, when, thankfully, shorts were introduced. Dress regulations are still in place to date, and in 2013, Wimbledon champion Roger Federer was asked to change his shoes because they had orange soles!

A woman tennis player who chooses to wear a non-white top or a low-cut top that displays too much cleavage is not allowed on court. Fashionistas beware! Also, if you have dark arm hair, the Club of England is well within its rights to ask you to bleach it white. Of course, it won't! But the worrying part is that it can.

The book *Tennis Fashions: Over 125 Years of Costume Change* by Valerie Warren mentions that the tradition of 'tennis whites' dates back to the 1800s. Tennis players wore white then to avoid sweat patches on their coloured clothing. The book states that this rule was imposed only on women initially because it was 'quite unthinkable that a lady should be seen to perspire'. Sexist, to say the least!

The rules have relaxed a wee bit at Wimbledon in recent years, though, to be fair. Tennis players do showcase designs that are bold and beautiful. Self-expression through attire is the new normal. In fact, tennis apparel has witnessed a fashion revolution of sorts over the years. This fashion evolution has been an amalgamation of fashion trends, along with technological advancements, to suit the needs of tennis players. Attire that was once restrictive has also evolved with the sport. Tennis apparel is now aimed to please, with comfort, mobility, and performance receiving equal importance, other than making a style statement. The love affair between tennis and fashion is an everlasting one, with celebrities from different fields watching the Grand Slams dressed in their splendid best. The tennis player is now a brand, and modern tennis clothing offers added advantages other than fetching those lucrative endorsement deals.

- Tennis clothing is now designed to keep sweat at bay so that players stay dry and comfortable during a strenuous tennis match.
- Modern tennis apparel offers UV protection, protecting players from the harmful rays of the sun.
- Tennis clothing is designed to give the player enough flexibility to move freely on the tennis court. Gone are the days of the prudish Victorian gowns!

ROYALTY

In 2003, the tradition of tennis players bowing or curtsying to members of the royal family, seated in the Royal Box, was discontinued. This was a practice whenever players entered or left the Centre Court. Now, players are required to bow or curtsy only if the queen or the Prince of Wales is present, as a mark of respect. There is no evidence to suggest that this curtsy was enforced in the early days when the queen made the famous 'kneecap' threat to whoever did not consume strawberries while watching the tennis.

WIMBLEDON IN POPULAR CULTURE

Strangely, tennis wasn't the only sport that brought national fame to Wimbledon. The Wimbledon Football Club won the prestigious FA Cup, beating Liverpool in 1988.

In 2004, a film called *Wimbledon* was released, starring Paul Bettany and Kirsten Dunst as tennis champions. Although hardcore tennis fans will find it tough to visualize, it was a charming romantic comedy with a tennis twist.

In 2005, Snoop Dogg and Justin Timberlake collaborated on the music single 'Signs'. The song features lyrics like 'You'll see Venus and Serena, in the Wimbledon Arena', referring to the Williams sisters. The lyrical leaning towards the Williams sisters is probably because the musical artists are American. They could have done a much better job with the lyrics, though. Scroll up to check out the lyrics of 'Anyone for Tennis' by Cream (the rock band, not the one had with strawberry) for some really cool lyrics.

Wimbledon is also the setting for the acclaimed novel *The War of the Worlds* by H.G. Wells.

AMAZING FACTS ABOUT WIMBLEDON

- The gentleman who won the 1879 Wimbledon championships was a vicar named J.T. Hartley. He was so unsure of his tennis abilities that he was positive he would lose in the first match itself. Well, the vicar was wrong for once, but the problem was that he had failed to arrange a substitute to cover his Sunday services while he won all his matches to lift the title. Losing my religion?

- Irish tennis player Vere Thomas 'St. Leger' Goold reached the 1879 Wimbledon men's Singles final only to lose to the vicar, John Hartley. But Goold has a record that's tough to beat, and it's doubtful if anyone would want to beat this record. He is the only Wimbledon finalist in history to have been convicted of murder. But it wasn't losing the Wimbledon final to a vicar that caused him to become a murderer. Twenty-eight years after he lost that final, Goold and his wife murdered a rich widow so that they wouldn't have to repay the money they had borrowed from her. Dangerous game of Mixed Doubles this!
- You've all heard of the Williams sisters in tennis. But have you heard about the Watson sisters? The first woman to become Wimbledon champion was Maud Watson, who beat her sister Lillian Watson in the final. Elementary, my dear!
- Since 1902, Slazenger has supplied tennis balls to Wimbledon. This collaboration, of being the official supplier of tennis balls to Wimbledon, is believed to be the longest in sports goods history.
- In 1905, May Sutton of the United States became the ladies' champion of Wimbledon, thus becoming the first overseas winner of the tournament. Nowadays, it's all about overseas winners, though.
- The year 1927 saw 15-year-old Sidney Wood become the youngest male to ever play Wimbledon. When he was 19 years old in 1931, Wood became the only tennis player to win Wimbledon by default when his

opponent in the final, Frank Shields, withdrew because of an injury. Shield's granddaughter is more famous even among tennis fans, though, and she goes by the name of Brooke Shields.

- On 11 October 1940, a bomb hit Centre Court in Wimbledon during World War II. The bomb dropped on a corner of the competitor's stand, and the damaged part was repaired only in 1947.
- In 1949, Wimbledon saw a strange sight in those days, as an American female tennis player, aptly named Gertrude 'Gorgeous Gussie' Moran, chose to wear a skirt that exposed her knees and revealed her frilly lace knickers. Convention at the time demanded that women wear knee-length skirts. Prudish Wimbledon officials complained instantly that she was bringing sin and vulgarity into tennis. Wonder what that hidebound bunch would have said seeing the skirts of some of the modern female tennis players today! But Moran became a household name thanks to her skirt style, rather than the fact that she was one of the better tennis players of her time. Although Gussie didn't win Wimbledon, she brought women's tennis into the spotlight.
- Martina Navratilova is the most successful women's Singles player in Wimbledon history in the Open Era, with 9 victories to her name. Steffi Graf and Serena Williams are second on this list with 7 wins apiece.
- Roger Federer is the man with the most Wimbledon men's Singles titles in the Open Era. The Swiss legend has won 8 Wimbledon crowns.

Roger Federer Remembers His Eight Wimbledon Wins

- The distinction of being the shortest player to play tennis at Wimbledon goes to Gem Cynthia Hoahing. She was an English female tennis player of Chinese heritage. She played tennis from the second half of the 1930s until the early 1960s. Hoahing was only 4 feet and 9 inches tall.
- The only male tennis player to ever win a Wimbledon Singles title while wearing glasses was Jaroslav Drobný in 1954.
- The unseeded Markéta Vondroušová became the lowest-ranked winner, at No. 42, when she won the Wimbledon ladies' Singles final in 2023, defeating Ons Jabeur. She also became the first unseeded player to win the Wimbledon women's Singles title.
- In 1907, Austrian tennis player Mita Klima became the youngest player ever to play at Wimbledon. She was only 13 years old, and although she exited in the first round itself, this was a stupendous achievement, to say the least.

- Richard Norris Williams was one of the lucky few to survive the sinking of the *Titanic*. But he had spent so much time in freezing water before he was rescued that the rescue doctor recommended that both his legs be amputated. Williams absolutely refused and recovered only a few months later to become the Wimbledon Doubles champion in 1920. You can't always trust the doctors, can you?
- Did you know that approximately 54,250 tennis balls are used every year at Wimbledon? That's about 24 cans daily for outside courts and 48 cans for show courts. If you are thinking that's too many balls, think again. These balls are inspected and replaced rather meticulously so that they are always in top condition. Balls at Wimbledon are changed after the first 7 games and then after each subsequent 9th game. When they are not in use, these tennis balls are placed in a refrigerated container so that their quality and bounce are maintained.
- Bet you didn't know that about 700 of these tennis balls conveniently go missing by the end of the tournament. Some of the spectators watching the match simply pocket the wayward balls that land in the stands and take them home as souvenirs. Who can blame them? It's Wimbledon, after all! But here's an interesting piece of information for those ball snatchers. You can buy a can of three tennis balls for £2.50 after Wimbledon is done with them. That's not a bad bargain, eh? Leave them balls alone!
- When Billie Jean King won her first Wimbledon title, she received a 25-pound gift voucher. Compare that

with Venus Williams's earnings, who received 300,000 pounds when she won.

- Wimbledon first offered prize money in 1968. Before that, strangely, there was no prize money.
- In 2007, the prize money for Wimbledon winners became equal for women and men after years of disparity.
- Wimbledon was cancelled in 2020 because of the Covid-19 pandemic. The last time Wimbledon was cancelled before that was in 1945, because of World War II.
- The youngest tennis player to win Wimbledon is the German player Boris Becker. He was a 17-year-old unseeded player when he won the title in 1985.
- Serbian tennis player Goran Ivanišević is the only winner of Wimbledon whose name has alternate consonants and vowels.
- Goran Ivanišević also had a killer serve. In 2001, he was ranked No. 125 in the world and was due for surgery on his left shoulder. Despite the overwhelming odds, he smashed an astonishing 212 aces en route to winning Wimbledon. He dished out 35 aces in the semi-final and served 27 more in the final. However, Goran Ivanišević's 212 aces in Wimbledon fell just short of the record for the most aces in a tennis tournament, which is held by John Isner. The man achieved the record for the most aces at the 2018 Wimbledon Championships.
- Wimbledon witnessed the longest tennis match in history in 2010 between John Isner and Nicolas Mahut. After the play ended after over three days of

tennis, lasting 11 hours and 5 minutes, both tennis players and the umpire were gifted a crystal bowl each and champagne flutes.

John Isner vs Nicolas Mahut | Wimbledon 2010 | The Longest Match in Full

- The shortest match in Wimbledon history lasted for just 20 minutes. This was a ladies' Singles match played between Susan Tutt and Marion Boundy in 1969. Susan Tutt wrapped up the match 6–2, 6–0.
- The fastest serve recorded in Wimbledon history was 153 miles per hour (246 km per hour), dished out by the Frenchman Giovanni Mpetshi Perricard in 2025. This broke the previous record at Wimbledon of 148 miles per hour, set in 2010 by the American player Taylor Dent.
- The fastest serve by a woman at Wimbledon was dished out in 2008 by Venus Williams at 129 miles per hour.

- Grunting has always been a part of sport. Monica Seles became famous for it. Russian female tennis player Maria Sharapova faced a lot of criticism for her grunting, with even the crowd chanting 'quiet please' in jest. During Wimbledon 2009, the Russian's grunt reached 105 decibels, setting a record for the loudest grunt then. Sharapova's grunt was louder than a motorcycle, a lawnmower, and even a small aircraft landing. It matches the volume of an ambulance siren and is just five decibels lower than the roar of a lion. But the funniest thing is that Sharapova is not the world's loudest grunter in tennis anymore. Her record was broken by Portugal's Michelle Larcher de Brito, a considerably lower-ranked player but definitely a better grunter. Her grunt has been recorded at 109 decibels at Wimbledon. Well, that's just one decibel lower than a lion's roar, so here's hoping that she'll roar like a lioness soon!
- The original Wimbledon winner's trophy is not taken home by the champions. Instead, it remains on display at the All England Club's museum. The winners are only given replicas of the official trophies. Thankfully, they can take the prize money home!
- Wimbledon has a unique environment management system that ensures that 8 litres of fresh and clean air for every individual is pumped into Wimbledon's bowl every second. The retractable roof over Wimbledon's bowl takes just 10 minutes to close.
- In 2023, Wimbledon introduced virtual reality (VR) and artificial intelligence (AI) for an immersive fan experience. Viewers could now immerse themselves in

tennis action from the comfort of their living rooms. Thanks to technology, fans who cannot get a ticket for the matches can get a similar experience sitting on their couches. Wimbledon has also made use of technology to introduce its first AI umpire, aptly named 'RoboRef' to make remarkably accurate line calls with the aid of computer vision and machine learning.

- During the Wimbledon Championships, a total of 3,000 staff serve about 2,34,000 meals to the players and guests throughout the course of the tournament. This includes 18,000 servings of fish and chips, 6,100 plates of pasta, 4,200 servings of sushi for the players only, 2,76,000 glasses of Pimm's, 1,92,000 strawberries, and 65,000 ice cream sticks. That's a lot of food! You can't play or watch tennis on an empty stomach, after all!

WIMBLEDON'S HAWK EYE

Rufus the Hawk is a famous Wimbledon celebrity! If you thought that's the nickname of a tennis player, you are as far from the truth as Rufus flies. Yes, Rufus is a real Harris hawk who has been employed by the Wimbledon authorities. Rufus's job might sound simple, but it's actually not.

Every morning before the matches begin, Rufus is released into the skies. He circles the sky above the Wimbledon grounds so that the local pigeons are scared and kept away. Rufus is trained not to harm these pigeons, but he ensures that they do not become distractions by landing on the tennis courts while play is on.

The protector of Wimbledon for more than 10 years, Rufus also has his own All-England Club ID card. But Rufus doesn't believe in taping himself to just one organization and is a consultant for various other high-profile clients, like Fulham Football Club, and Westminster Abbey. Realizing his true worth, Rufus has been requested to pass on his knowledge and skills to the next generation. He is busy training new hawks like Pollux on how to get used to TV cameras and equipment.

In 2012, there was panic in England when Rufus the Harris's hawk was stolen. Thankfully, he was returned by the thieves, who were probably tennis fans as well. No wonder Rufus has more than 10,000 followers on X (previously Twitter). Rufus rocks! Fly like Rufus!

Rufus – The Real Hawk-Eye

4

THE GRAND SLAMS – II

THE FRENCH OPEN

Roland-Garros (French Open) Logo

The French Open, or Roland-Garros, is officially called the Internationaux de France de Tennis. It is one of the four Grand Slams and the only one that's played on a clay surface. It has been named after French aviator and hero Eugène Adrien Roland Georges Garros, who passed away during World War I in 1918 while engaging in aerial combat. He was a close friend of Émile Lesieur, president of Stade Français. To honour his friend's memory, Lesieur named the new stadium after him when it was inaugurated in 1928.

Apart from being a fighter pilot, Roland Garros was also a pioneering French aviator, whose accomplishments included the first solo flight across the Mediterranean Sea. He is also famous for putting a machine gun through the propeller of a fighter plane. Eugène Adrien Roland Georges Garros was also more interested in football, rugby, and cycling than tennis. But that's a different story.

The stadium was built in his name to host the final of the Davis Cup, as the French team was a potent force in international tennis at the time. Known as the Four Musketeers, the French tennis team boasted of players like Jean Borotra, Jacques Brugnon, Henri Cochet, and René Lacoste. No wonder the trophy that is awarded to the winner of the men's Singles event has been named the Coupe des Mousquetaires, or the Musketeers' Cup, as a tribute to the four legendary musketeers of French tennis who ruled over the French Open till 1933 and dominated world tennis between 1926 and 1932.

However, the Coupe des Mousquetaires, which has been awarded since 1981, doesn't leave the stadium, and winners of the French Open are given a smaller replica to take home. No one can question this decision as the trophies are made of pure silver and designed by Maison Mellerio dits Meller, the oldest jeweller in Paris. The silver bowl is, in turn, decorated with a vine-leaf frieze at the top and has two lovely swan-neck handles. A marble base serves as a mount for the trophy, on which the names of all the previous winners are embossed. In fact, the trophy is so valuable that it is kept in a special trunk that was created by Louis Vuitton.

> French jewellery house Mellerio dits Meller was founded in 1613 and is active to date. It's the oldest family-owned jewellery company in Europe. The famous Mellerio cut is a 57-facet jewel cut, oval-shaped, within an ellipse.

In time, the Roland-Garros Stadium was slowly extended and modernized and now hosts a Grand Slam that's famous globally and is unique enough to stand out from the rest. What began as France's defence of the Davis Cup today hosts the second prestigious Grand Slam of the tennis season, after the Australian Open. Roland-Garros is a premier clay court championship held between late May and early June every year. It boasts of 17 courts, with a 15,000 spectator capacity for each court, and is a great tennis experience for sure. But players need unique skills and tremendous stamina to play on the slow surface of clay courts, which requires them to play longer rallies than on other surfaces.

The tournament has been held in the French capital, Paris, with periodical regularity since its inception in 1891. The only exceptions were the years between 1915 and 1919, because of the outbreak of World War 1, and in 1940, because of World War II.

In 1891, the tournament was held at different venues, like the Stade Français, the Parc de Saint-Cloud, and the Racing Club de France's Croix-Catelan grounds. The star of the times or the king of clay in that era was a gentleman named Max Decugis, who really maxed it out by winning 8 titles between 1903 and 1914.

However, one must keep in mind that Big Max played only against players belonging to French clubs. 1925 saw a major change in the history of the French Open when foreign players were allowed to participate. This was the actual birth of the 'French Open'. In the initial days, the French dominance continued, and this was the golden age of French tennis. Between 1920 and 1926, Suzanne Lenglen triumphed six times and was the first tennis celebrity in the true sense of the word.

World War II brought about a halt to the proceedings, and English-speaking tennis players started winning the French Open instead of the French-speaking ones. The wave began with the Americans, and then came the Australians, with big guns like Rod Laver, Ken Rosewall, and Margaret Court dominating the court. After the ushering in of the Open Era or professional tennis in 1968, new stars like Björn Borg and Chris Evert created an impact. 1979 saw the first expansion of the Roland-Garros Stadium as the courts were increased from five to ten. The second extension took place in 1986, and the third extension happened from 1992 to 1994. This brought Roland-Garros to its present size of 8.5 hectares, which had

20 tennis courts ensconced within it, featuring two show courts aptly named Philippe-Chatrier and Suzanne-Lenglen.

The French did offer some resistance to the foreign dominance of Roland-Garros, with wins by Françoise Dürr in 1967, Yannick Noah in 1983, and Mary Pierce in 2000. But the 1990s saw the invasion of the Spanish Armada as Paris was ruled by players like Arantxa Sánchez, Sergi Bruguera, Carlos Moyá, Albert Costa, and Juan Carlos Ferrero. Then arrived the greatest of them all, and his name was Rafael Nadal.

It's interesting to note that clay courts were created in the late 19th century when British professional tennis player William Renshaw was sick and tired of watering his grass court.

> William Renshaw is regarded as one of the early great innovators of tennis, as well as a grandmaster of tennis strategy. Thanks to his experiments and innovations, as well as his exciting brand of tennis, several new tactics emerged, such as the conventional modern serve, the volley, and the overhead smash. Today, these are the weapons modern tennis players use on the court to win matches.
>
> He won 12 Wimbledon titles: 7 in Singles and 5 in Doubles. The Doubles titles were all won in partnership with his twin brother, Ernest Renshaw. The period of their dominance in the late 19th century was called the 'Renshaw Rush'.

The courts at Roland-Garros need a lot of clay. To achieve this, the raw material is obtained first by extraction

William Renshaw (L) with His Twin Brother Ernest Renshaw (R)

from natural quarries. This is then baked in ovens at a temperature of 800°C before it is crushed. Each track has a requirement of 500 kg to 1,000 kg of clay annually. The clay is changed daily when the tournament is in progress. Each day, an amount of between 100 and 150 kg of new clay is used. The Phillipe-Chatrier court requires a total of 1.5 tons.

But did you know that the clay surface that we see at the French Open is technically not clay? The courts are actually surfaced with white limestone, coal residue, and gravel. A cover of powdered red brick dust is then applied to it, giving it its reddish colour. About 44,000 kg of crushed red brick is used annually to create the courts of the French Open. Let's take a closer look at the clay court composition of Roland-Garros. The surface is composed of many layers:

- The top layer: This consists of a thin layer of crushed red brick that makes up the typical reddish hue of the surface.
- The middle layers: These are a blend of white limestone and clinker, which make the court stable and provide the much-needed bounce.
- The base layer: This layer is composed of 30 cm of crushed gravel, which makes the court durable.
- The drainage layer: This ensures that optimal conditions are maintained on the court after rainfall.

Interestingly, the first French Championship that was played in 1891 was on sand, which is difficult to fathom now. For the first six years since its inception, the French Open was open only to men, and that, too, only to the members of French tennis clubs. Women were only allowed to participate from 1897, and it took as long as 1925 for the tournament to be fully open to all, when non-French tennis club members were allowed to participate.

In 1968, when the Open Era of tennis began officially as amateur tennis players competed with professional tennis players, the French tournament became the first Grand Slam to go open. The French Open was also the first tournament that offered equal prize money to men and women, and this began in 2007.

The Stade Roland Garros features a complex that spans 34 acres and has 20 courts. Court Philippe-Chatrier is the cherry on the cake and houses over 15,000 spectators. The Suzanne-Lenglen show court was constructed in 1994. The women's Singles trophy is also named after the legendary Suzanne Lenglen and has been awarded since 1979. Lenglen was the winner of 31 major titles between 1914 and 1926 and won the French Open 6 times. The court named after her has a seating capacity of over 10,000. In 2019, a third show was made, which was named after Simmone Mathieu, tennis champion and leader of the French Resistance, which fought against Nazi Germany during World War II. This has a seating capacity of just 5,000.

Since 1989, the Jacques-Brugnon Cup has been given to the winners of the men's Doubles in the French Open. The trophy is dedicated to the memory of Jacques Brugnon, a master of men's Doubles, who won the men's Doubles title 5 times at Roland-Garros.

The Simonne-Mathieu Cup has been given to the winners of the ladies' Doubles at the French Open since 1990. This oval trophy has two small swan-shaped handles and water-leaf mouldings. The trophy is a fitting tribute to the clay-court specialist and French patriot Simonne Mathieu, who played in the 1930s. She won the French Open Singles title twice and reached the final 8 times. She also won 8 titles in women's and Mixed Doubles. In 1940, Simonne Mathieu joined the forces of General de Gaulle in London and served as a captain before the war ended.

Jacques-Brugnon Cup

The Marcel Bernard Cup has been awarded at the French Open since 1990 to the winners of the Mixed Doubles event. The trophy is a tribute to French player Marcel Bernard, who triumphed at Roland-Garros in 1946. He also served as president of the Féderation Française de Tennis (FFT), the French Tennis Federation, which is the governing body for tennis in France.

Sadly, French tennis has not witnessed its past glory in recent years. The last male French player to win the French Open was Yannick Noah, who won the tournament way back in 1983 by defeating Swede Mats Wilander in the final. Incidentally, Noah is the only Frenchman to date who has lifted the title in the Open Era since 1968. Bit of a lonely Noah's ark story this.

Even the women's scene is nothing to write home about, as Mary Pierce won way back in 2020 by beating Spaniard Conchita Martínez. French hopes now rest on Arthur Fils in the men's Singles and Loïs Boisson in the women's Singles. But you can bet that even the most die-hard French fan won't bet on them. However, miracles have happened in tennis before, and maybe there'll be one at Roland-Garros, too. Remember Andy Murray at Wimbledon?

But then again, this is not the easiest surface to play tennis on, a fact that many top tennis players have discovered. The ball tends to bounce slower and higher than on other surfaces like grass or a hard court, resulting in longer points and rallies. This makes the French Open rather excruciating and demanding for a player. One cannot dominate a match simply by serving well and following it up with volleys and strong ground strokes. Thanks to the slowness of the surface, opponents have plenty of time to recover and bounce back into the game. Players like Rafa, who are quick on their feet and have a wider variety to their game, have a higher chance of winning. That's why modern tennis legends like Pete Sampras were unsuccessful on the clay courts of the French Open. Players with big serves and suited to a fast style of play often don't perform as well on the clay courts of Roland-Garros as they do on hard courts and grass courts. Pete Sampras was noted for his big serve and his precise volleys, which helped him win 14 Grand Slam titles. But he could never win the French Open, where his best performance was reaching the semi-finals in 1996. He's not the only one in this club, as great tennis players like Frank Sedgman, Bill Tilden, John Newcombe, John McEnroe, Jimmy Connors,

Maria Bueno, Stefan Edberg, Boris Becker, Lleyton Hewitt, Louise Brough, Virginia Wade, and Martina Hingis have never managed to win at Roland-Garros despite winning several Grand Slam titles. John McEnroe and Stefan Edberg will be particularly distressed, as both of them reached the French Open Finals only once in their illustrious careers to lose in five-set battles.

In comparison, tennis players like Björn Borg, Ivan Lendl, Mats Wilander, Chris Evert, Gustavo Keurten, Rafael Nadal, Monica Seles, and Justin Henin have performed better at this tournament because of their adaptability to slower tennis courts. In the Open Era, Jan Kodeš, Rod Laver, Björn Borg, Andre Agassi, Roger Federer, Rafael Nadal, and Novak Djokovic are the only male players who have won both the French Open and Wimbledon, where the surfaces are vastly different. Björn Borg is the classic example of versatile tennis talent as he has won the French Open and Wimbledon thrice in a row, and that, too, with a wooden racket.

Talking about tennis players, let's take a look at them from the lens of the French Open.

- Spaniard Rafael Nadal, or Rafa, has won the most men's Singles titles at the French Open. He has 14 wins at Roland-Garros between 2005 and 2022, which makes it even more spectacular. Known as the 'King of Clay', Rafa is the most successful player on this surface, and his achievements will continue to inspire generations of tennis players. His uncanny abilities of speedy court coverage, tenacity to play long rallies, and a powerful forehand with a mysterious topspin have unsettled and upset his powerful opponents.

- Chris Evert is the most successful women's Singles player in French Open history in the Open Era. She has won 7 titles between 2005 and 2022. Steffi Graf is a close second with 6 titles.
- In women's Doubles, Martina Navratilova has the maximum wins with 7 French Open titles.
- In men's Doubles, Australian Roy Emerson has the most titles, with 6 Roland-Garros wins.
- American Michael Chang became the youngest male player to win the French Open Singles title in 1989. Chang was 17 years and 3 months old when he won the title. Seeded 15, Chang beat top tennis players like No. 1 Ivan Lendl and Pete Sampras to reach the finals, where he met the Swede Stefan Edberg. The final was an epic battle of five sets, in which Michael Chang emerged triumphant.
- The oldest male to lift the French Open title is Spanish player Andrés Gimeno, who was 34 years and 10 months when he won in 1972.
- In 1990, Serbian–American Monica Seles became the youngest female champion of the French Open. She was only 16 years and 6 months old when she upset No. 1 seed Steffi Graf in straight sets in the final to lift the title.
- Serena Williams is the oldest woman to win the French Open. When she won in 2015, she was 33 years and 8 months old.
- Fabrice Santoro and Arnaud Clément played the longest match in French Open history in 2004. The

marathon duel went on for 6 hours and 33 minutes. In this first-round match at the French Open, Fabrice Santoro defeated Arnaud Clément after a battle that went on for two days. The final score read 6–4, 6–3, 6–7 (5), 3–6, and 16–14.

- The longest rally in professional tennis took place at Roland-Garros in 1984. This was during a match played by French tennis players Jean Hepner and Vicky Nelson. As many as 643 shots were exchanged in this lengthy rally, which went on for 29 minutes and 43 seconds.
- Roger Federer heaved a huge sigh of relief when he won the elusive French Open title in his career in 2009 by beating Robin Söderling in the final. This was the only French Open title the Swiss star managed to win, but it completed his Career Grand Slam title as he had won all three other Grand Slams prior to this victory. With this win, Federer also equalled Pete Sampras's record of 14 Grand Slam titles and became the sixth man in tennis history to win all four Grand Slams.

As per its policy of promoting gender equality in tennis, the French Open has been offering equal money to male and female players since 2007. The tradition continues, and the prize money has also witnessed a considerable increase over the years. The 2024 edition of the French Open offered €53.48m in prize money, equivalent to USD56.58m. This went up to €56.352m in 2025. The prize breakdown for the tournament in 2025 is as follows:

Men's Singles Winner	€2,300,000
Women's Singles Winner	€2,300,000
Men's Singles Runner Up	€1,150,000
Women's Singles Runner Up	€1,150,000
Men's Doubles Winners	€580,000
Women's Doubles Winners	€580,000
Mixed Doubles Winners	€122,000
Men's Singles Semi-Finalists	€600,000
Women's Singles Semi-Finalists	€600,000
Men's Singles Quarter-Finalists	€380,000
Women's Singles Quarter-Finalists	€380,000

The tennis players who have raked in the moolah at the French Open include:

- Rafael Nadal: With a mind-boggling 14 titles at Roland-Garros, Rafa sits on top of the biggest money-makers of the French Open.
- Chris Evert: She has 7 Roland-Garros titles to her name and is second on the list.
- Novak Djokovic: Third on the list, having won the title thrice.

TOO MANY BALLS

About 65,000 balls are used for the French Open, which goes on for two weeks. Until 2020, Babolat was the official ball of Roland-Garros. After that, Wilson established itself as the official brand.

RAMASSEURS DE BALLES

The ball boys and ball girls who serve at the French Open are called 'ramasseurs de balles'. Almost 4,000 children apply for the training programme, and they are between 12 and 16 years old. The requirements to make the cut are certainly demanding. They cannot be taller than 1.75 m and must possess clear vision. That means no glasses or contact lenses. After careful selection, only 250 to 300 children make the final cut to become ramasseurs de balles at the French Open. They work in teams of six, with two of them in a crouching position outside the court at the net and four of them standing at the back of the court. They work on a rotational basis to prevent exhaustion during the match. After the end of the tournament, ball kids are allowed to keep their kits as souvenirs. The kit of a ball boy/girl consists of a pair of shoes, two pair of socks, two shirts, two pairs of shorts, and one tracksuit.

One of the most memorable and funny images in the French Open revolving around a ball boy was during a game in 2014. Novak Djokovic was playing a match when it started raining. He invited one of the ball boys who was carrying an umbrella to sit with him. He exchanged the boy's umbrella for his racket, offered the boy a bottle of sparkling water, and the two ended up toasting. This was a great gesture from a tennis champion to appreciate the efforts of a ball boy, which brought about laughter from a bored audience because of the rain stoppage. Djokovic received a standing ovation from the crowd.

French Open in the Rain with Novak Djokovic and the Ball Boy – Roland-Garros 2014

THE VENUE

Roland-Garros has a complex of 21 acres with 21 tennis courts, a restaurant, a garden, a bar complex, and a multimedia museum that features a history of tennis. Compared to the 46.5 acres of the US Open, 42 acres of Wimbledon, and 100 acres of the Australian Open, the French Open might be the smallest venue among all Grand Slams. But it is also the most accessible to travellers and tennis fans because of its proximity to the city centre of Paris.

A DAY AT THE FRENCH MUSEUM

The Musée de Roland-Garros at the Roland-Garros stadium was built in 2003 and houses about 14,000 collector's items and documents that narrate the history of the Roland-Garros Stadium, as well as the history of French tennis. Fans can relive tennis history here thanks to memorabilia, documents, and archive footage. You can take a look at the different tennis outfits worn by tennis players through the ages and trace the evolution of tennis rackets and other sports equipment. The various cups and trophies displayed here are also worth a visit.

AMAZING FACTS ABOUT THE FRENCH OPEN

Once upon a time, the French Open was played on grass courts. This was from its inception in 1891 till 1907. From 1908, the changeover was made to clay, which is the chosen surface to date.

The French Open is the only Grand Slam that begins on a Sunday. Clearly, the French don't believe in weekends when it comes to sports.

The first African-American to win Roland-Garros was Althea Gibson, who won the title in 1956 by beating the defending champion, British tennis player Angela Mortimer, in the final, and that, too, in straight sets. Gibson's triumph was not only a major upset in tennis, but also a great historic landmark for the African-American community. With the intention of breaking more barriers for African-Americans, Althea Gibson also focused on golf and basketball. Amazingly, she turned professional in both those sports as well.

The fastest Grand Slam final took place at Roland-Garros. In 1988, German superstar Steffi Graf faced Natasha Zvereva of Belarus in the French Open final. The match lasted just 34 minutes, with Graf blowing away her rival 6–0, 6–0. That's quicker than the time it takes me to find my house keys every morning!

Any mention of Roland-Garros is incomplete without Rafael Nadal, because of his impressive record here. Rafa has won more than 90% of the sets he has played here. He's had to play a five-set match at Roland-Garros only thrice out of about 115 matches played here, and Rafa won all 3 times. The first was against American John Isner in 2011, and the second was against Serbian Novak Djokovic in 2013. This match was termed as the peak of the Nadal–Djokovic rivalry, and some commentators called it the best match ever to be played on clay. The third encounter took place in 2022, against Canadian Felix Auger-Aliassime, who was coached by Rafa's uncle, Toni Nadal, at the time. Toni knew Rafa's game so well that the less-fancied Canadian coached by him managed to stretch the Spaniard to five sets. But Rafa emerged victorious despite his uncle's tactical genius and his opponent's strong fightback.

Nadal vs Djokovic 2013 Men's Semi-Final | Roland-Garros Classic Match

Rolex at Roland-Garros

The name Roland-Garros conjures up images of people wearing a brand of clothing that's typical of the French Open. The brand Lacoste is synonymous with the tournament, particularly the caps and polo shorts and tees. The brand is named after René Lacoste, a French tennis player and businessman. The most famous of the four French musketeers, Lacoste was also an inventor who was much ahead of his time. Once, in 1923, his team captain promised to gift him a crocodile leather suitcase if Lacoste won his tennis match. Although Lacoste failed to win the bet, he was nicknamed 'the crocodile' by the American press because of his resilience on the tennis court. The nickname spread like wildfire in tennis circles, and Lacoste was actually proud of it. He even had a crocodile embroidered on his shirts and blazers. This became the logo for Lacoste's sportswear brand and is an iconic symbol today. Lacoste is a great fashion brand today and is a favourite among tennis players and sports fans alike.

Another iconic brand that has forged a strong relationship with tennis, and Roland-Garros in particular, is Rolex. In 1978, Rolex began its tennis journey by becoming the official timer of Wimbledon. But today, Roland-Garros is the ramp walk of Rolex, with the biggest tennis players sporting the iconic brand on their wrists. Swiss legend Roger Federer was the most prominent ambassador of Rolex, even though his French Open record is nothing to write home about. But it's the thought that counts, and Rolex is the watch that ticks all boxes.

5

THE GRAND SLAMS – III

THE US OPEN

US Open Logo

The US Open is the fourth and final Grand Slam in the calendar year. It usually begins on the last Monday of August every year and continues till the second Sunday of September. The US Open is not just a tennis tournament but a true celebration of sports, history, and culture. This is the place where legends are made. It is perhaps fitting that it is the last Grand Slam of the year. As American tennis fans are fond of saying, 'We saved the best for the last.'

It all began in 1881 as a men's tournament played on grass courts with the Newport Casino in Rhode Island as the venue. But only the members of the US National Tennis Association were allowed to participate. No surprise that there were only 25 male tennis players who competed against each other. Richard Sears was crowned the first champion of this tournament, which is now known as the first US Open after the Open Era. But the tournament was then known as the US National Championships.

In the final, Richard Sears defeated William Glyn 6–0, 6–3, 6–2 to clinch the inaugural title. The rules were a wee bit strange, as all the matches leading to the final were played as the best of three sets. However, the final was best of five sets. Can you believe that in its early days, this tournament originally took place on a grass court in the garden of one of the organizers? A few years later, there was a logical shift in venue as you really can't host a tennis tournament in someone's garden. In 1917, during World War I, the US Open was called the Patriotic Tournament.

1968 saw the name of the competition change from the US National Championships to the US Open. This was in tune with the advent of the 'Open Era', when professionals were allowed to compete with amateurs for the first time. This also led to the name US Open. The first US Open Singles champions in the Open Era in 1968 were American Arthur Ashe and British tennis player Virginia Wade.

In 1970, the US Open became the first Grand Slam tournament to introduce the tie-break when a set ended at 6 games all. 1975 saw another first at the US Open, as it became the first Grand Slam tournament to host night matches under lights. The US Open switched from grass courts to clay courts for just a three-year period, between 1975 and 1977. Then, the shift to hard courts took place in 1978, and that has been a constant to date. By 1978, the tournament had also shifted to the USTA National Tennis Center in New York. This venue has hard courts, which became the preferred surface for the US Open after clay. From 1978 onwards, the matches at the US Open have been played on this hard-court surface, which is covered with 'DecoTurf' artificial grass.

The US Open thus became the only Grand Slam that has been played on three different surfaces – on grass, clay, and its present form, hard court. The popular name is Flushing Meadows – which is the home tennis arena for the US Open.

It was only in 1887 that women were allowed to participate at the US Open. From 1887 to 1918 for women, and from 1884 to 1911 for men, champions of the tournament had it quite easy in the next year's tournament thanks to a challenge round system. The defending champion automatically qualified for the final of the tournament and waited for the challenger, who would be chosen after the other candidates battled it out to reach the final.

In the pre-Open era before 1968, Molla B. Mallory won the most US Open titles in women's Singles, with 8 wins to her name. Post 1968, in the Open Era, Chris Evert and Serena Williams are tied, with 6 titles apiece. It remains to be seen if anyone can break Mallory's impressive record in the future. In men's Singles in the pre-Open Era, three players are tied with 7 US Open titles each. They are Bill Larned, Richard Sears, and Bill Tilden. After 1968, three tennis players have the maximum US Open titles. Jimmy Connors, Roger Federer, and Pete Sampras are all tied with 5 wins each.

Chris Evert is the only woman tennis player who has managed to win the US Open on two surfaces, clay and hard court. Jimmy Connors went a step ahead, as he has won the US Open title on all three surfaces: grass, clay, and hard court, becoming the only tennis player in history to do so.

Chris Evert

Jimmy Connors

2005 witnessed the introduction of blue inner courts and green outer courts at the US Open to make the ball easier to sight for the players and officials. 2006 saw the introduction of the Hawk-Eye system at the US Open, another first in a Grand Slam. Using this revolutionary technology, players could challenge line calls made by the chair umpire or the line judges.

AMAZING FACTS ABOUT THE US OPEN

The US Open is the only Grand Slam where matches are scheduled regularly at night. This decision was enforced from 1975 to enable more tennis fans to watch the matches after returning from work in the evening. Also, the lights used at night create an atmosphere that's electrifying and spectacular to add to the tennis excitement.

The Arthur Ashe Stadium, which hosts the US Open, is the largest tennis stadium in the world. The stadium has a seating capacity of more than 23,000 and has been named after Arthur Ashe, the first African American male to win the US Open title.

The Arthur Ashe Stadium is a part of the USTA Billie Jean King National Tennis Center. This massive complex has 22 courts at Flushing Meadows.

In the late sixties and the seventies, Billie Jean King was a top female tennis player. Apart from winning the famous Battle of the Sexes, we also need to thank Billie for reducing the pay disparity that existed between male and female tennis players at the US Open and in tennis as a whole. When Billie Jean King refused to play and threatened to boycott the event unless this was achieved, the US Open offered equal money to male and female players in 1973, becoming the first Grand Slam to set an example that the others followed in due course. Tennis also became the first sport to offer equal compensation to winners of both sexes. In an apt decision, the US Open complex was renamed the USTA Billie Jean King National Tennis Center in 2006 in honour of Billie Jean King. The iconic tennis player won four US Open Singles titles in 1967, 1971, 1972, and 1974.

She also won the title in Doubles and Mixed Doubles and has a total of 7 US Open titles in all categories.

Billie Jean King

The fans at the US Open in the sixties and seventies were also entertained by some of the biggest musical superheroes. In 1964, the Beatles famously landed at the Forest Hills Stadium in a helicopter to perform. Folk legend Bob Dylan performed here in 1965 and took a break for 51 years before performing at the venue again in 2016. That's longer than a tennis career. The times they are a-changing, babe.

The term 'Super Saturday' also originated in the US Open. This was a sort of tradition from 1984 to 2007, in which the semi-finals of the men's and women's matches took place in one marathon Saturday. Sounds like Saturday night tennis fever!

Joe Hunt was the winner of the 1943 US Open title. Unfortunately, that was the last tennis match he played. Because of World War II, Hunt could not get leave from the US Navy in 1944 to defend his US Open title. Tragically, the tennis and war hero was killed in an airplane crash in February 1945.

Ball boys and ball girls have to undergo a rigorous selection process for the US Open. This includes tests for speed, agility, and precision. However, there is no age restriction for a ball person at the US Open.

In 2006, the US Open became the first Grand Slam tournament that used Hawk-Eye technology to review line calls made by the umpire and line judges.

In 2008, the US Open launched a campaign to support sustainability, keeping in mind its impact on climate change. This green initiative featured recycling, lighting that was energy efficient for the nocturnal matches, and the use of recycled materials to print tickets and for use in other event needs.

In 2020, in a first, the US Open was held without any fans in the stadium because of the Covid-19 pandemic. It was postponed until September, but fans were still entertained, albeit in isolation. No wonder the US Open generates the most revenue among all the Grand Slams.

Wimbledon might be the most prestigious, but the US Open is more profitable.

The player payout isn't too bad either. In 2025, total player compensation stood at $90 million. This is the largest payout in the history of tennis and a substantial increase of 20%, as total compensation in 2024 was $75 million.

Fancy a drink after watching those players sweat it out at the US Open? Try the Honey Deuce! That's the official cocktail of the US Open. The concoction has lemonade, Grey Goose vodka, Chambord liqueur, and ice, garnished with four honeydew melon balls. Strange brew?

Since 1987, Tiffany & Co. has been the official producer of the US Open Trophy awarded to the men's and women's Singles champions. This trophy that tennis players dream of getting their hands on is 18 inches in height and weighs 10 pounds.

The prize money that comes with the trophy is a big deal. The US Open recreated history in 2025 by becoming the first tennis event to offer $90 million in total prize money. This is the largest prize money in tennis history, eclipsing the $75 million offered in 2024, which was also the previous record. That's an increase of 20% from 2024. Out of this purse, the men's Singles champion and the women's Singles champion earn $5 million for winning 7 matches each, an increase of 38.89% from 2024. The runner-up received $2,500,000, again an increase of 38.89%. However, the substantial percentage increase drops significantly for the initial rounds of the US Open. First round losers earn $110,000, which is an increase of 10% from 2024. Not bad for playing one match in the main round and losing it as well. Since 2015, the US Open prize money has increased by a mind blowing 113%. No wonder we are witnessing a growing interest in tennis worldwide, as parents try to push their kids early into the sport. Anyone for tennis? You bet!

STRAIGHT FACTS SERVED UP ABOUT PLAYERS AT THE US OPEN

- In 1887, Ellen Hansel became the first female Singles winner of the US Open.
- At 16 years and 8 months, Tracy Austin was the youngest US Open Singles champion in 1979. She defeated Chris Evert in the final.
- The youngest men's champion in the US Open is Pete Sampras, who lifted the title in 1990 when he was 19 years and 28 days old. Sampras defeated fellow American Andre Agassi in the final in straight sets.
- The oldest man to win the US Open was Bill Larned, who won 7 Singles titles. The last of these titles came in 1911, when Bill was 38 years, 8 months, and 3 days old. Not bad for an old timer, eh?
- When Serbian great Novak Djokovic won the US Open in 2023, he was 36 years and 111 days old. That made him the oldest men's Singles winner in the Open Era. Novak is still going strong, though, and could better this record.
- Novak Djokovic created a new infamous record in 2020 at the US Open. He became the last player in tennis history to be disqualified from a Grand Slam after he accidentally hit a line judge with a ball due to his frustration at losing a point.

- The record for the oldest Singles champion is held by Norwegian–American Molla Bjurstedt Mallory. In 1926, she won the title aged 42 years and 5 months. That's even better than good old Bill Larned.
- Molla Bjurstedt Mallory and Bill Tilden each played in as many as 10 finals of the US Open, even though they did not win them all. Tilden played the finals between 1918 and 1929 and won 7 Singles titles. Mallory reached the finals between 1915 and 1924 and in 1926 to win a record 8 US Open titles.
- As they say famously in sport, it's not about winning but taking part. Well, that's certainly applicable to Vic Seixas Jr. The American tennis player has participated in an astonishing 28 US Opens. So what if he managed to win only once! Vic Seixas Jr. won the US National Championship (the name for the US Open then) in 1954. But his participation in so many US Opens would have made Vic Seixas Sr. proud surely.
- Martina Navratilova has played a record 21 consecutive US Opens from 1973 to 1993, which is a testament to her extraordinary fitness and skill levels. Navratilova has a better record at the US Open than Vic Seixas Jr., though, as she has won 4 Singles titles in 1983, 1984, 1986, and 1987.
- Martina Navratilova also became the third woman in US Open tennis history after she won the rare 'Triple Crown' in the 1987 US Open. This means that she won not only the Singles title, but the Doubles, as well as the Mixed Doubles titles. The only other women who have achieved this extraordinary feat are Margaret Court and Billie Jean King. Who said you can't have it all?

Martina Navratilova

- In 1968, Arthur Ashe became the first and only African American to date to win the US Open. This feat not only earned him a place in the record books, but also a stadium in his name. In 1997, the stadium used for the US Open inside the USTA National Tennis Center was named the Arthur Ashe Stadium. In 2016, a retractable roof was added to the stadium. This is the largest tennis stadium in the world, with a seating capacity of 23,771 spectators, and is divided between three viewing levels. It is a fitting tribute to Arthur Ashe's legacy.
- Arthur Ashe's legacy expands way beyond the tennis court, as he was a leading civil rights activist and humanitarian. The stadium has been named in his honour both for his singular achievement in tennis, as

well as to serve as a constant reminder of the impact of his humanitarian efforts.

- American tennis great Jimmy Connors has won the US Open Singles title 5 times, in 1974, 1976, 1978, 1982, and 1983. But the icing on the cake is that he's the only one to win the US Open on all three different surfaces: grass in 1974, clay in 1976, and hard court in 1978. Jimmy Connors also holds the record for playing in the most consecutive finals of the US Open as a male player. He reached the final five times in a row from 1974 to 1978. In 1991, Jimmy Connors made an unbelievable comeback after undergoing wrist surgery and dropping down the rankings table. Aged 39 and ranked 174, Connors was written off by tennis experts as way past his prime. But he proved everyone wrong as he had a magic run at the US Open, including a five-set comeback win against Aaron Krickstein in the fourth round. Kriskstein was two sets up and serving for the match at 5–2. But it was Jimmy Connors' 39th birthday and his last waltz at the US Open. The passionate and partisan American crowd was cheering him on. The old fox gathered courage and bounced back from a two-set deficit and a tricky 2–5 fifth-set hole to win the match. Sadly, this magic run ended in the semi-finals, where Jimmy Connors lost in straight sets to fellow American Jim Courier. No wonder Jimmy Connors called the 1991 US Open 'the best 11 days of my playing career'.
- Serena Williams won the US Open women's Singles title on 11 September 1999. She became the first African American woman since Althea Gibson to

win a Grand Slam title. The very next day, Serena partnered with her elder sister, Venus, to win the women's Doubles title as well.

- In a first in 2001, Venus Williams and Serena Williams became the first sisters to meet in the final of the US Open and also at any Grand Slam event. Sadly, the epic moment lasted for only 69 minutes as Venus beat her younger sister in straight sets, 6–2, 6–4.
- The longest match recorded in US Open tennis history took place on 12 September 1992. The historic men's Singles semi-finals between Swede Stefan Edberg and American Michael Chang went on for 5 hours and 26 minutes. Edberg emerged as the winner of this epic encounter 6–7, 7–5, 7–6, 5–7, 6–4. After this hard-fought victory, Edberg prevailed over Pete Sampras in the final, beating the American in a 4-setter, 3–6, 6–4, 7–6 (7–5), 6–2, to earn his second US Open title and sixth and final Grand Slam Singles title.
- Britain's Emma Raducanu achieved the rare feat of becoming the first qualifier in the Open Era to win a Grand Slam in tennis. She did this at the US Open in 2021. What was amazing was that she did not lose a single set in the tournament.
- The other two women who have won the US Open title in the Open Era as unseeded players, apart from Emma Raducanu, are Kim Clijsters of Belgium in 2009 and American Sloane Stephens in 2017. By winning her first of 3 US Open titles in 2009, Kim Clijsters became the first mother to win a Grand Slam in almost three decades.

- The only unseeded man to win the US Open title in the Open Era was American tennis player Andre Agassi in 1994. The last unseeded player to achieve this feat was Fred Stolle, who won the US Open in 1966, two years before the championship was open for both amateur and professional tennis players, thus ushering in the Open Era.
- The youngest men's Doubles champion of the US Open is Vincent Richards. In 1918, he was just 15 years, 5 months, and 8 days old when he won the title. Now, that's a record that won't be easily beaten today.
- The record for the most US Open Singles titles in the Open Era is jointly held by Jimmy Connors, Pete Sampras, and Roger Federer, who all have 5 titles each.
- It's a tie between Serena Williams and Chris Evert for the most women's Singles titles in the Open Era. Both have won 6 US Open titles each. Steffi Graf is a close second with 5 titles.
- The record for winning the most men's Doubles titles at the US Open is held by the American twins Bob and Mike Bryan, who have won 5 men's Doubles titles.
- Louise Brough and Margaret du Pont had a great pairing at the US Open when it came to women's Doubles. This great duo won 12 US Open titles between 1940 and 1957. That's longevity and success combined for you!
- The longest tiebreak at the US Open took place during the 2012 US Open men's Singles final. In a face-off between Serbian tennis player Novak Djokovic and British player Andy Murray, the first set went into a

massive tiebreak, which Murray won 12–10. Andy Murray went on to win this thrilling contest that stretched to five sets 7–6, 7–5, 2–6, 3–6, 6–2.

- When it comes to the latest finish in US Open history, there are actually three. Interestingly, all three of these matches finished at 2.26 a.m. New York time. The first match was a five-set marathon that was played for four hours in 1993 between the two Swedes, Mats Wilander and Mikael Pernfors. The second match that tied this record was played in 2012 between Philipp Kohlschreiber and John Isner. The third was in 2014, the match between Milos Raonic and Kei Nishikori.
- The US Open has been dominated by American tennis players over the years. There have been 85 American male champions in US Open history and as many as 93 titles for American women tennis players in Singles. Of course, out of the 85 men's Singles titles, 66 came in the amateur era, where very few professional players participated. But 19 titles came in the Open Era, post 1968. American tennis players Jimmy Connors and Pete Sampras have 5 US Open men's Singles titles each. Both Chris Evert and Serena Williams have won the US Open women's Singles title 6 times.

AMAZING FACTS

Player in Focus: John McEnroe

American John McEnroe is considered one of the greatest tennis players of all time and has been inducted rightly into the Tennis Hall of Fame. He made his US Open debut as an 18-year-old in 1977.

John McEnroe

Before he began his stellar tennis career, McEnroe was a ball boy at the Forest Hills Stadium, where he watched legends at play, like Pancho Gonzales and Adriano Panatta. He even served Björn Borg as a ball boy and was a huge fan of the Swedish legend before becoming his greatest rival. But McEnroe was keener to follow in Borg's footsteps because he generated a lot of interest from young girls.

In an unusual incident at the 1977 US Open, a gunshot interrupted proceedings during a match played between

Eddie Dibbs and John McEnroe. There was a huge commotion in the crowd as it was discovered that a tennis fan had been hit in the leg by a stray bullet fired from outside the ground. The fan must have missed the match that continued soon after, which McEnroe won in an upset. But the 18-year-old McEnroe failed to win the tournament, which was his US Open debut. McEnroe confessed it was a bizarre first US Open for him.

Although John McEnroe lost in the fourth round in his debut US Open in 1977 to 1975 US Open champion Manuel Orantes, he bounced back in the years to come by winning 3 US Open titles back to back in 1979, 1980, and 1981. He became the first man to achieve this feat since Bill Tilden in the 1920s. America had discovered its new tennis superhero. John McEnroe did not disappoint, as he won his fourth US Open Singles title in 1984. He has a total of 7 Grand Slam Singles titles, having won Wimbledon thrice.

McEnroe was a versatile tennis player who was also a master in Doubles. He won 9 Grand Slam titles in men's Doubles, which included 4 US Open titles and 5 Wimbledon titles. Peter Fleming was the Doubles partner McEnroe tasted the most Grand Slam success with. They won 57 Doubles titles together, including 7 Grand Slam victories. The duo won the US Open thrice and Wimbledon four times. John McEnroe also won Grand Slam Doubles titles with other partners, winning the US Open with Mark Woodforde and Wimbledon with Michael Stich.

John McEnroe also won the French Open in Mixed Doubles, teaming up with Mary Carillo. Among the Grand Slams, only the Australian Open is missing from his trophy room. He played in the Australian Open just five times in his entire career. In 1983, he lost in the semi-finals. In 1990, McEnroe looked a strong contender, with a No.5 world ranking.

John McEnroe was a genius on the court when facing formidable rivals like Björn Borg, Jimmy Connors, and Ivan Lendl. But his great tennis play was often eclipsed by his explosive temper. While this made him a fan favourite, it also earned him the tag of 'Superbrat' by the British press when he was just 20 years old. McEnroe was notorious for arguing with umpires and linesmen and abusing them.

AGAINST ALL ODDS: HOW GABRIELA SABATINI WON THE US OPEN

Gabriela Beatriz Sabatini was an Argentine former professional tennis player who was the heartthrob of millions of boys and men across the world. However, Sabatini was also one of the leading women's tennis players from the mid-1980s to the mid-1990s. She won 41 titles in both women's Singles and women's Doubles in a career that was eclipsed by legends like Martina Navratilova and Steffi Graf. Sabatini was ranked World No. 3 in both Singles and Doubles. Interestingly, Sabatini has won only one Grand Slam final, in which she upset Steffi Graf, and has won just one Grand Slam women's Doubles final, where she partnered with Steffi Graf to win the 1988 Wimbledon title. But the manner in which Sabatini won her maiden Grand Slam Singles title was enough to earn her a place in the International Tennis Hall of Fame in 2006.

As 1989 ended, Sabatini found herself ranked No. 3 in the world in women's Singles, with the legends Martina Navratilova and Steffi Graf ahead of her. Despite all her efforts, a Grand Slam title remained elusive for the 19-year-old Argentine player. In 1990, Sabatini began working with an eminent sports psychologist named Jim Loehr to change her style of play and win a Grand Slam title. Loehr advised Sabatini to express herself better in the heat of the tennis match by being more aggressive and displaying signs of emotion, like a fist pump or exclaiming in joy. This seismic change of personality was still not enough, as Sabatini lost in the Round of 16 at the French Open despite being seeded No. 4 at the tournament.

A change in the coaching regime followed as long-time coach Ángel Giménez made way for Carlos Kirmayr. A part-time drummer in a band named Fleabags, Kirmayr encouraged Sabatini to look beyond tennis to express herself better on court. Sabatini started taking French lessons, played frisbee on the beach, and bought a camera to become an amateur photographer. Kirmayr insisted this would expand her vision and help her become a better tennis player.

Kirmayr also made Sabatini aware of the strengths she had displayed when she had partnered with Steffi Graf to win the Wimbledon Doubles title. Her reach, volley skills, and on-court agility were brilliant, and her new coach worked around these strengths. He bought a hand-held VCR and made Sabatini study her strengths by making her watch her old games.

When Sabatini faced Steffi Graf in the final of the 1990 US Open, hardly anyone expected the Argentine to win. In

21 previous encounters between the two, the mighty Graf had won 18 times. But this match saw the emergence of a new Gabriela Sabatini. Even before the match, Gaby said, 'If Steffi wins, it will be because she wins, not because I lose.'

Gabriela Sabatini

Sabatini stunned Graf in the first set and won it 6–2. Then, she found herself serving for game, set, match, and title in the second set at 5–4. But Steffi Graf made a characteristic comeback by breaking Sabatini. The second set led to a tiebreaker at 6–6. Sabatini was down 5–6 in the tiebreaker, and Steffi needed just one point to take the second set and force the match to the deciding third set. But Sabatini played like a woman possessed and saved 2 set points to go up 7–6 in the tiebreak. Now, she was just one point away from winning the second set and the match to achieve her first Grand Slam win. Sabatini won the point with a forehand that shot past Graf and slumped to the ground. She had beaten Steffi Graf for the fourth time in her life, and that, too, in a Grand Slam final in straight sets 6–2, 7–6.

This was one of the best US Open finals for sure and a classic example of how an underdog managed to defeat a champion by realizing the need to change and actually being bold enough to make those changes.

A MISOGYNYSTIC TRADITION?

It's common knowledge that women play a best of three sets in tennis while men play a best of five sets match. One of the main reasons given for this inequality in terms of work hours on the court, especially since the pay is equal now, is that this is to meet the logistical challenges to maintain the current format of tennis. Adding five-set matches for tennis would increase the duration of the tournament, create scheduling hassles, and increase costs.

But why should women play three sets and men play five sets when there is pay parity now? One has to go back to the origin of the best-of-three format to understand this. Even then, chances are we won't. From 1891 to 1901, women participated in best-of-five matches in the US

National Championships, now known as the US Open. No one complained, not even the women tennis players, who were also getting less money than the men. But for some strange, inexplicable reason, an organization called the United States National Lawn Tennis Association Council decided to shorten the women's matches to a best-of-three sets format. This body was composed totally of male members, who unanimously deduced that playing five sets would be too physically taxing for women. The body of men with strong opinions did not heed what the female players thought about this, including two-time champion Elisabeth Moore. She argued that women were fully capable of playing and enduring five-set matches. She was right, of course, but what is baffling is how this strange tradition has continued in tennis to date for more than a century. Tennis legends like Billie Jean King have long advocated for five-set matches for women, but to no avail.

In our modern world, where equality of the sexes and competition is stressed upon in all spheres of life, women deserve to compete in sport just like men. The wonderful sport of tennis shouldn't be an exception just because a patriarchal body decided that that's the way things should be. If it upsets the scheduling, maybe we should have it in the semi-finals and finals to see which way the wind blows. Bring back the five-setter in women's tennis!

6

THE GRAND SLAMS – IV

THE AUSTRALIAN OPEN

Australian Open Logo

Organized by Tennis Australia every year at Melbourne Park in Melbourne, Victoria, the Australian Open is the first of the Grand Slams in chronological order. It kicks off the exciting tennis action for the entire year. The Australian Open sets the stage for the annual Grand Slam tennis action and is followed by the French Open, Wimbledon, and the US Open, respectively.

1904 saw the creation of the Lawn Tennis Association of Australasia with the objective of ensuring participation for Australia in the Davis Cup and for the nation to host the regional championships. In 1926, the name changed to the Lawn Tennis Association of Australia. Sir Norman Brookes became the president and served for 29 long years. In 1927, the organization changed its name to the Australian Championships. After the Open Era was declared, the final name change happened in 1969, when the tournament was renamed the Australian Open as a symbolic reference to the Open Era of tennis.

Even though tennis players from all around the world participate in the Australian Open today, this was not the case when it began in 1905. Known as the Australasian Championships then, it was a major challenge for international players to participate in the tournament because of the lack of jet travel and the amount of time it took to get to the island from Europe and America. In the 1940s and 1950s, when air travel boomed, the Australian Open attracted top players from all continents. The first edition of the tennis tournament was held at the Warehouseman's Cricket Ground in Melbourne. It was played on grass courts, and only 17 players took part. The first men's Singles champion was a gentleman named Rodney Heath. Thanks to Melbourne's obsession with cricket, which still continues, Australian tennis had to share a home with cricket in the initial years. Howzat?

Thankfully, the Melbourne Cricket Ground and Melbourne Park have both become iconic venues. However,

Melbourne was not the only city to host the Australian Open in its early years, unlike now. The tennis tournament was hosted by a different Australian city every year, and it took place in Sydney, Adelaide, Hobart, Brisbane, and Perth, among other Australian cities, and was also held in Christchurch, New Zealand.

In 1972, the Australian Open found a new home in the Kooyang Lawn Tennis Club in Melbourne after sharing space with cricket for a long time. Melbourne was the chosen city for the home of Australian tennis simply because it had the maximum number of tennis spectators or fans. In 1988, the Australian Open was given a permanent address at Flinders Park by Tennis Australia, the governing body of Australian tennis. It is famously known as Melbourne Park today.

The Australian Open did not take place for eight years since its inception in 1905. This was on account of World Wars I and II, and the tournament was not played between 1916 and 1918, and again between 1940 and 1945. The Lawn Tennis Association of Australia became a company in 1984, realizing the need for tennis to flourish in Australia as a sport. In 1986, the company began to trade as Tennis Australia (TA). TA is also the governing body of tennis in Australia. It aims to promote the sport by conducting both domestic and international tournaments, like the Federation Cup, Davis Cup, and of course, the Australian Open.

1988 witnessed a dramatic transformation in the playing surface of the Australian Open. Prior to this, the tennis tournament had been played on grass. Now, the Australian Open has shifted to hard courts. This major transformation not only changed the style and speed of tennis played here but also ushered in a new era that intended to stay abreast of the evolving dynamics of modern tennis. The blue hard court surface is a characteristic feature of the Australian Open. Initially, Rebound Ace was used as the surface, which was later changed to the blue Plexicushion we see today. The faster surface offers a more consistent playing experience, attracting tennis players from across the globe.

1988 also witnessed the Australian Open receiving an expensive makeover of 70 million dollars. The old Kooyong Stadium was abandoned as the state-of-the-art Flinders Park took its place.

The men's Singles winner at the Australian Open received the Norman Brookes Challenge Cup, named after the great Australian former champion. The Daphne Akhurst Memorial Cup is awarded to the winner of the women's Singles title. During the 1920s, Daphne Akhurst won the tournament five times.

In 1982, the Australian Open saw just five tennis players from the top 30 in the table attending the event. That's less than 20% of top talent, and it was clearly the worst edition of the tournament. This forced the organizers to sit down and do a serious rethink about the scheduling and the prize money on offer, which were the two areas of discontentment for players. Travelling to Australia during the festive season was a no-no for many players. Why would someone want to play tennis on Christmas Day, after all?

In another erratic and erroneous move, there were two tournaments in 1977 but none in 1986 because of the calendar complications from December 1985 to January

1987. So, 'Who won the Australian Open in 1986?' is the perfect trick question in a sports quiz show.

Before 2001, women received less prize money than men in the Australian Open. Forty years ago, this pay disparity was most striking, as female athletes were paid three times less than their male counterparts. The gender gap kept lessening as the years went by, and finally, in 2000, both males and females were given the same amount of prize money in a landmark move.

The Australian Open has also hiked the total prize money considerably in recent years to attract the top players and compensate them better. In 2023, the total prize money went up to AU $76.5 million, which was an increase of 3.4% from 2022. In 2024, this went up by a further 13% as the prize pool was AU $86.5 million. The men's and Singles champions now received AU $3.15 million each. This was much needed for the players as the cost of training, coaching, and other elements crucial in tennis had also risen considerably.

AMAZING FACTS ABOUT THE AUSTRALIAN OPEN

- Until 1946, the Australian Open was only about local players competing for the title. This was when foreign players, especially players from the USA, began arriving by plane to participate in the Australian Open. Earlier, the same trip by sea was cumbersome as it took 45 days to reach Australia. The 1946 American Davis Cup team of Jack Kramer, Ted Schroeder, and Frankie Parker set the trend and was the first to fly into Australia. They defeated Australia 5–0 and flew back in style with the Davis Cup.

- The tournament is played in extreme heat. Temperatures at the Australian Open are known to soar above 40°C or 104°F. The Australian Open has taken several steps to tackle this extreme heat and protect the players and officials. The Extreme Heat Policy enforced at the Australian Open features the closure of the retractable roofs of the arenas when the heat is on. Sometimes, play has also been suspended because of extreme temperatures. When the temperature soars above 40°C, play at the Australian Open is usually stopped. The summers in Australia are particularly harsh, and the extreme weather conditions make it tough for players to maintain their energy levels in a tennis match and keep themselves hydrated. In 2019, the Heat Stress Scale (HSS) was introduced at the Australian Open. This is basically a 5-point scale measuring the impact of heat on the players. The HSS takes into account factors like humidity, temperature, wind speed, and of course, radiant heat to make this assessment. Player cooling and recovery measures are then put into place after the assessment. These include:

Expanded breaks for the players, like a 10-minute break for women after playing the second set, if the match extends to a third set and the HSS is at a high level. Similarly, men are given a break after the third set if the match extends into the fourth set.

Hydration support is given to the tennis players on court with water and electrolyte drinks served.

Ice towels are made available courtside to the players, who can cool off after a long rally, tiring game or during a changeover.

Cooling stations are on offer with fans, shade, and misting systems around Melbourne Park.

- In 2020, the record for the highest attendance at a Grand Slam event was set at the Australian Open. A total of more than 8,12,000 fans gathered to watch tennis, which just goes to show how seriously the Aussies take their sports. This record was smashed by the Australian Open again in 2024 as a mind-boggling 10,20,763 fans attended the event.
- The Australian Open boasts of a main court known as the Rod Laver Arena, with a capacity of more than 14,000 spectators. Named after Aussie tennis legend Rod Laver, it is an iconic tennis stadium.
- The Australian Open also became the first Grand Slam to boast of a retractable roof. In a remarkable example of innovation, the Rod Laver Arena at Melbourne Park became the first stadium in a Grand Slam to have this feature. Now, matches could continue in inclement weather or when it was too hot to play. Soon, the other stadiums, like Margaret Court Arena and John Cain Arena, also had retractable roofs. The Australian Open is the only Grand Slam that has three stadiums with retractable roofs.
- The Australian Open uses about 50,000 tennis balls for every tournament. More than 300 ball boys and girls are selected to volunteer on the tennis courts.

The attendance of tennis fans is normally so high at Melbourne Park that they consume approximately 1,60,000 ice creams and 75,000 hot dogs. Strawberries are not fashionable at the Australian Open, unlike Wimbledon.

- The Australian Open has earned the nickname of the 'Happy Slam' thanks to its warm hospitality, great infrastructure, and friendly, passionate fans. The atmosphere to play tennis can't be any better. The fact that this term was famously coined by tennis legend Roger Federer speaks volumes about the Australian Open.
- The term 'Happy Slam' is rather apt to describe the Australian Open, which extends into a cultural extravaganza from a tennis tournament. As players and fans from all over the world congregate to celebrate quality tennis, a melting pot of cultures is formed and celebrated. This brings about a festive feel to the Australian Open, which is similar to a summer festival. Melbourne Park is transformed into a hub of entertainment, with live music and food stalls being the perfect icing on the cake.
- The table format of the Australian Open changed as many as seven times between 1969 and 1988. Sometimes, there were 48 players, and sometimes, there were 64 after the knockout rounds were over. There was no fixed number. The present format of 128 players was only enforced in 1988, after the tournament shifted to Flinders Park.

AMAZING FACTS ABOUT TENNIS PLAYERS AT THE AUSTRALIAN OPEN

- In 1922, the first Mixed Doubles event was held at the Australian Open, which was won by the Australian pair Jack Hawkes and Esna Boyd. The popular event is hosted to date. Interestingly, another Australian duo, of Olivia Gadecki and John Peers, won the Mixed Doubles title at the 2025 Australian Open.
- The youngest tennis player to win the Australian Open is former Swiss tennis player Martina Hingis. She lifted the women's Singles title in 1997 when she was only 16 years and 3 months old. This is amazing considering that Hingis turned pro when she was 15, and just a year later, she won a Grand Slam title. Dreams do come true at the Australian Open.
- The oldest tennis player to win the Australian Open is Ken Rosewall. The Australian was 37 years and 2 months when he won the Grand Slam event.
- The tennis player who has won the most Australian men's Singles titles is Serbian great Novak Djokovic, with an astonishing 10 Australian Open Singles titles. If Novak manages to win another Australian Open title, he will become only the third player in tennis history to bag more than 10 titles in a Grand Slam tournament. The first to do so was Margaret Court, with 11 Australian Open titles under her belt, and the second is Rafael Nadal with 13 victories at the French Open.

- Since the beginning of the Open Era, American Serena Williams has won the most women's Singles titles, with 7 Australian Open wins.
- Unlike American players who have dominated the US Open, Australian tennis players haven't managed to replicate this success on local turf. The last Australian male to win the Australian Open was Mark Edmondson, way back in 1976, and it's interesting to note that he defeated fellow Aussie John Newcombe in the final. In fact, the last time we saw an Aussie play the men's Singles final at the Australian Open was in 2005. Australian tennis fans were hoping Lleyton Hewitt would break the jinx, but he lost against Russian Marat Safin in that final.
- But as they say, there's always light at the end of the tunnel. 2022 saw the Aussies celebrating as local girl Ashleigh Barty became a national hero. She famously won the Australian Open women's Singles title by defeating American Danielle Collins in the final in straight sets. Aussie tennis fans celebrated in pubs as this ended a 44-year drought.
- When it comes to women's tennis at the Australian Open, here's an interesting stat. Since 2000, only three non-seeded female players have managed to reach the final at the tournament in women's Singles. But only one of them managed to win the title. They are Serena Williams in 2007, Belgian Justine Henin in 2010, and Spaniard Garbine Muguruza in 2020. Serena Williams became the first non-seeded player in 29 years to win the Australian Open, when she beat No. 1 seed, Russian Maria Sharapova, in straight sets (6–1, 6–2)

in the 2007 final. In the 2010 final, Serena beat Justine Henin in a three-setter in the final. In 2020, Garbine Muguruza lost to Sofia Kenin in the final.

- The last time the Australian Open women's Singles final was played between players of the same nationality was in 2017. The American ladies were the famous Williams sisters – Serena and Venus! Serena emerged triumphant in this battle by beating her elder sister, Venus, 6–4, 6–4.
- The 2012 men's Singles final at the Australian Open is renowned for being the longest Grand Slam final in tennis history. This epic battle between Novak Djokovic and Rafael Nadal went on for 5 hours and 53 minutes. That's almost six hours of quality tennis! Djokovic got the better of Nadal in this encounter in a marathon five-setter 5–7, 6–4, 6–2, 6–7, 7–5.

Novak Djokovic vs Rafael Nadal Full Match | Australian Open 2012 Final

- The record for the highest win percentage at the Australian Open during the Open Era also belongs to

Novak Djokovic. With 82 wins and 8 losses, it stands at an impressive 91.1%.

- Japanese female tennis player Naomi Osaka has an 85% win rate at the Australian Open, having won 22 matches here and lost just 4. Only two other women have a better win rate than her at the Australian Open during the Open Era. Both are American tennis players. The first is Serena Williams, with 89%, and the second is Jennifer Capriati, with 90%.
- In another first at any Grand Slam, Swede Joachim Johansson smashed 51 aces in a match against American Andre Agassi in the 2005 Australian Open. This was the first time that someone served more than 50 aces in a single match. However, even this was not enough for Johansson to win against his tough opponent, as Agassi prevailed in 4 sets. This record has been broken elsewhere after that by players like John Isner, Nicolas Mahut, and Ivo Karlović. But it still holds good at the Australian Open.
- Miracle winners at the Australian Open refer to those players who came back from the brink of defeat to win the tournament. These players saved one or more match points before they won the Australian Open. John Newcombe did it in 1975, Stefan Edberg did it in 1985, and Marat Safin did it in 2005. But the king of all miracle winners is Australian Gerald Patterson, who won the title in 1927. Patterson saved as many as an astonishing 7 match points in the fourth set of the final he played against John Hawkes.

- The 1972 Australian Open final almost didn't happen because of a lack of player attendance. Australian tennis player Ken Rosewall was stuck in traffic en route to the stadium. Thankfully, he hitched a ride with a motorcyclist to arrive on time. This motorcyclist had no idea he was taking the famous Ken Rosewall to the stadium and mistook him for a tennis fan going to watch the final. Ken and the art of motorcycle maintenance?
- Tennis is never boring with Boris Becker around. The Australian Open witnessed this in 1991 when the German won the title after beating Ivan Lendl in the final. But after the handshake with his rival at the end of the match, the German player simply disappeared and turned up at the award ceremony. Explaining his brief disappearance, Boris Becker said he had gone to swim in the Yarra River alone for a few minutes. That's quite a water-y celebration!
- The Australian Open has strict rules when it comes to insulting the public. Players have been fined for this offence in the state of Victoria until the mid-eighties, after which, no one has done such a thing. Even local players are not spared, as the angry young Australian man Pat Cash discovered early on in his career. He was met at the exit by police officers, who had received complaints about Cash's behaviour from television viewers. In 1981, a linesman left his position right in the middle of New Zealander Chris Lewis's Doubles match, complaining that Lewis was being boorish.

THE BIGGEST CONTROVERSIES AT THE AUSTRALIAN OPEN

The Australian Open is no stranger to controversy. Some of the biggest controversies in tennis have been witnessed on these courts. Here are the top five controversies to plague the Australian Open.

- **The Deportation of Novak Djokovic:** All eyes were on the big Serbian, Novak Djokovic, before the 2022 Australian Open. He had been the most successful male tennis player at the Australian Open, with a record 9 titles. Would Djokovic secure his tenth in a tournament that had been so kind to him? Well, Djokovic's luck ran out just when he needed it most. It turned out that he was deported from Australia and not allowed to play in the Australian Open after he confessed that he was not vaccinated against Covid-19. Strict Australian laws demanded that everyone entering the country must be vaccinated. To his dismay, Djokovic discovered that his visa had been cancelled by the Australian Border Force. He was also subject to the humiliation of being detained in an immigration detention hotel for a few days. Djokovic appealed the decision in the court as it was a personal choice to get vaccinated, and the decision ruled in his favour. But Djokovic's visa was cancelled again by Alex Hawke, the then minister of Immigration, Citizenship, Migrant Services and Multicultural Affairs of Australia. Hawke used his special powers to deny the nine-time Australian Open champion entry to Australia on 'grounds of health and good order'. Djokovic applied for a judicial review again, but this application was also dismissed. He had to leave Australia as a result. Even after winning 9 titles, Australia did not become the Serbian's second home and was definitely not a Happy Slam for him in 2022. Djokovic replied in style the very next year by winning his record tenth Australian Open title. Poetic!

- **The Default by John McEnroe:** In 1990, 30-year-old American John McEnroe took on Swede Mikael Pernfors in the fourth round of the Australian Open. This was a crucial year for McEnroe as he was trying to bag his first Australian Open title, which had eluded him thus far.

McEnroe made headlines in the 1990 Australian Open, but for all the wrong reasons. He became the first player to be disqualified for misconduct in a Grand Slam after 27 long years. The last tennis player to hold this infamous record was Willie Alvarez of Spain, in the 1963 French Open. Alvarez was set up against Martin Mulligan in a second-round match when he was disqualified for arguing with the umpire. But McEnroe's case makes Alvarez's default look like a petty crime. In the fourth round, he played Mikael Pernfors of Sweden. McEnroe won the first set easily, 6–1, but Pernfors raised his game to win the second set 6–4. During a changeover in the third set, McEnroe stood and glared at a lineswoman, who he thought had made a bad call and bounced a ball on his racket. He received a conduct code violation for unsportsmanlike conduct from the chair umpire, Gerry Armstrong.

But McEnroe won the third set 7–5. In the fourth set, McEnroe found himself down 2–4, and that's when fresh trouble erupted. McEnroe hit a forehand that went wide and threw his racket on the ground in disgust, and it bounced on the hard court. He smashed his racket hard at his next error, and this time, the racket's head cracked open. McEnroe received a second violation by Armstrong for racket abuse, to which McEnroe responded with verbal abuse. He was so loud that both spectators and television viewers could hear him. He received a third and final code violation.

'Default Mr McEnroe. Game, set, match,' Armstrong announced to the crowd of 15,000, which rose to their feet in unison, booing Armstrong and cheering for McEnroe. John McEnroe looked stunned as he stood with his hands on his hips. Then, he covered his face as reality dawned fully on him. McEnroe's jinx at the Australian Open continued.

- **The Medvedev–Tsitsipas Quarrel:** The rivalry between Russian tennis player Daniil Medvedev and Greek tennis player Stefanos Tsitsipas is legendary. This rivalry began at the 2018 Miami Open, and since then, these two have always tried to outdo each other on the tennis court. But when the two clashed at the 2022 Australian Open, no one could have predicted what was about to be served up. Medvedev took the first set and had the upper hand in the match. But trouble brewed as he lost his cool and started shouting at the chair umpire, asking him to stop Tsitsipas's father and coach from giving him instructions from the box. Grand Slams do not allow on-court coaching as a rule. Medvedev went on to win the match in a tense four-setter and went to the final. But the Greek wasn't pleased at all after the match. Stefanos Tsitsipas claimed that he was targeted by the umpires after Medvedev's false claims that he was being coached from the box. This led to a lot of controversy, which eventually died down after Medvedev lost in the final to Spaniard Rafael Nadal in a thrilling five-setter. Rafa clinched his second Australian Open title, as well as a then all-time record 21st Grand Slam Singles title.

- **Australian Bushfires:** During 2019 and 2020, Australia was ill-affected by bushfires that spread across the land. The 2020 Australian Open suffered as well, with many players complaining of breathing issues. Female tennis player Dalila Jakupovi had severe breathing problems that forced her to retire from the match. There were concerned calls that the tournament should be postponed or even cancelled. But the tournament went on despite the bushfire controversy.
- **The Match-Fixing Controversy:** Fresh controversy erupted during the 2016 Australian Open when rumours of match-fixing began doing the rounds. Before the tournament even began, reports indicated that as many as eight players in the main draw had been investigated for match-fixing. When the tournament began, unusual betting patterns were observed on a major betting site during the first-round Mixed Doubles clash between Lara Arruabarrena and David Marrero and Andrea Hlavá ková and Łukasz

Kubot. Betting for the match was suspended. Both the players and organizers denied any involvement in match-fixing, and the Australian Open continued despite the controversy.

7

THE ATP MASTERS, THE OLYMPICS, AND THE DAVIS CUP

THE ATP TOUR MASTERS 1000

The ATP Tour Masters 1000 is made up of a total of nine tournaments, which are played annually. These are top-tier tennis tournaments and are also called the 'Big Titles' of tennis. The ATP Tour Masters 1000 is ranked just below the Grand Slams in terms of prestigious tennis titles. The winner of each tournament is awarded a thousand points, and that explains the 1000 added to the name of the series. The nine tournaments in the series are:

- The Canadian Open, in either Toronto or Montreal, Canada.
- The Italian Open, hosted by Rome, Italy.
- The Indian Wells Master, also known as the BNP Paribas Open, in Indian Wells, California, USA.
- The Miami Open at Miami, USA.

- The Rolex Monte-Carlo Masters at the Monte-Carlo Country Club at Roquebrune-Cap-Martin, France.
- The Mutua Madrid Open at Madrid, Spain.
- The Cincinnati Open at Ohio, USA.
- The Rolex Shanghai Masters at Shanghai, China.
- The Rolex Paris Masters in Paris, France.

The 'Big Titles' are played on different surfaces. Eight of these tournaments are played on outdoor courts, while one is played on indoor courts. Five of the ATP Masters 1000 tournaments, including the Indian Wells Masters, the Miami Open, the Rolex Shanghai Masters, the Canadian Open, and the Cincinnati Open, are all played on hard courts. The Rolex Monte-Carlo Masters, the Mutua Madrid Open, and the Italian Open are the three tournaments played on clay courts. The Rolex Paris Masters is played indoors on hard courts.

AMAZING FACTS ABOUT THE ATP MASTERS

- Serbian great Novak Djokovic has won the most Singles titles at the ATP Masters, with a mind-blowing 40 titles. Apart from winning the most titles, Djokovic is the only tennis player in history to have achieved the 'Career Golden Masters'. This means that he has won each of the nine Masters event at least once in his career.
- In the Doubles event at the ATP Masters, the Bryan brothers, Bob and Mike Bryan, have won a record 39 titles. The American Bryan brothers are the only Doubles players to have completed the Career Golden

Masters, apart from Canadian Daniel Nestor, who has won it with multiple partners.

- The Rolex Monte-Carlo Masters was completely dominated by Rafael Nadal during his playing days on his favourite surface – clay. Nadal has won 11 Singles titles here, including an impressive 8 straight titles between 2005 and 2012.
- The oldest male tennis player to win an ATP Masters title is Indian Rohan Bopanna. He became the oldest Masters winner by winning the Doubles title at the 2023 Indian Wells title when he was 43 years old by partnering with Australian Matthew Ebden. Bopanna broke Daniel Nestor's record, who had achieved the feat as a 42-year-old in 2015. Bopanna repeated the feat by winning the 2024 Miami Open again with Matthew Ebden. Rohan Bopanna has won 6 Doubles titles at the Masters 1000.
- The Rolex Shanghai Masters is the sole tournament where no tennis player has won their first Masters 1000 title. The two Masters first-time finalists at the Shanghai Masters are Roberto Bautista Agut, who lost to Andy Murray in 2016, and Borna Coric, who lost to Novak Djokovic in 2018.
- American tennis player Jim Courier holds the record of winning the most Masters 1000 titles without losing a final. By winning the 1993 Rome Masters, Courier won his fifth Masters title in as many attempts. He became the only player to win his first 5 Masters title matches. Nikolay Davidenko is the only other player to have a perfect record in the Masters finals after

Rohan Bopanna

playing multiple times. The Russian has played three finals and won all of them.

- Only two male tennis players have won the 'Double Crown' at the Masters 1000, which means they have won both the men's Singles title, as well as the men's Doubles title, in the same Masters tournament. They are American Jim Courier, who did it in the Cincinnati Open in 1991, and Spaniard Rafael Nadal, who achieved the feat at Monte Carlo in 2008.
- The list of women who have managed to win the 'Double Crown' at the Masters 1000 is considerably

bigger. Nine women have managed to achieve this. Martina Hingis did this four times in her career at different venues. Martina Navratilova, Arantxa Sánchez Vicario, and Lindsay Davenport have done it thrice. Monica Seles, Mary Pierce, Conchita Martínez, Anastasia Myskina, and Vera Zvonareva have all won the 'Double Crown' once.

WHAT ARE ATP AND WTA RANKINGS, AND HOW DO THEY WORK?

Rankings of tennis players are reflective of how good their form is and how good they are performance-wise on the court and in tournaments during that period. Tennis rankings also decide the qualification of a player or players for an official or major tournament and determine player seedings during a tournament. This also decides the draws for the tournaments.

Initially, there was no formal ranking system in tennis for a long time. In the 1950s, popular British newspapers decided to take matters into their own hands and began issuing their own rankings. The most popular among these was famous tennis journalist Lance Tingay's annual list, which everyone in tennis circles looked forward to. This list of the top 10 tennis players was considered the ultimate list.

In 1972, the Association of Tennis Professionals, famously known as the ATP, was formed. This was the governing body for men's tennis in the world. For the first time, formal computerized tennis rankings were established to make the entry criteria perfect in an official tennis tournament. On 23 August 1973, the first official men's

Singles rankings were published. The first official ATP men's Singles world No. 1 was Romanian tennis player Ilie Năstase. The first men's Doubles tennis rankings took three more years to publish, and this was done on 1 March 1976.

Women's tennis refused to be left behind, and famous tennis player Billie Jean King formed the Women's Tennis Association (WTA) in 1973, which is the body that governs women's tennis in the world.

So, ATP rankings rate the men's Singles and Doubles players, and the WTA rankings grade the women's Singles and Doubles players. However, formalized rankings do not exist for Mixed Doubles.

When these rankings were first established, they averaged the results of all the players to rate them. Post 1990, this changed to a 'best of' system, and this system forms the core of the ranking that we know and follow today. While ATP rankings are based on the points the players earn in official tournaments that are ATP-certified in a time frame that is 52 weeks, this does not necessarily mean that a tennis player playing more tournaments will have an advantage in terms of rankings. A cap on the number of tournaments gets counted when rankings are formed. This number increased from 14 events to 18 in 2000 and then to 19 events in 2021. So, if a player plays in 21 tournaments in the 52-week period, his best 19 results are taken into consideration in his ranking system, which is 'the best of'.

Players can best improve their rankings by performing well in the four Grand Slams, eight compulsory ATP Masters 1000 tournaments, and seven other best results from either the ATP Cup, ATP Tour 500, 250, ATP Challenger Tour, or ITF WTT men's events. Other than the

Monte-Carlo Masters, participation in all the other eight ATP Masters 1000 tournaments is mandatory for players.

As the Monte-Carlo Masters is not a compulsory event, it does not need the top players to participate in it. This decision was made in 2009, when the entire tennis circuit was being overhauled and was done so that players had more flexibility in their busy calendar. April to July is a hectic period on the ATP tour, and skipping this clay tournament gives players a chance to rest and spend some quality time with their loved ones. Many American players opt to play in the ATP 250 tournament in Houston, which takes place at the same time and is less strenuous than the Monte-Carlo Masters. However, even though the Monte-Carlo Masters is not a mandatory event, the points still hold good for a player's ATP rankings. Other than this factor, why players still opt to play at the Monte-Carlo Masters is because it is the first major clay-court tournament of the season. This makes it perfect to prepare and warm up for the big daddy of clay – the French Open.

Before the year draws to a close, the ATP Finals are held, where the top eight ranked Singles and Doubles players participate. This gives them an extra tournament to improve their 'best of' rankings and also serves as a motivator for other players to try and break into the top eight to be eligible to play the ATP Finals.

Of course, the points awarded to each player vary from tournament to tournament, keeping in mind the history, prestige, and quality of participation. The four Grand Slams are the highest graded tournaments in the ATP tennis calendar. Winners receive 2,000 points, runners-up get 1,200 points, and semi-finalists receive 720 points.

The points keep decreasing as the levels decrease, with the qualifiers receiving 25 points. If a player wins the ATP Finals, he can earn a maximum of 1,500 points if he is undefeated during the tournament, which involves three round-robin matches as well.

In comparison, the winner of an ATP Masters 1000 tournament gets 1,000 points, while the runner-up receives 600 points. The points keep decreasing for the levels below, as the semi-finalists receive 360 points and the qualifiers 25 points. The winner of the ATP Tour 500 gets 500 points, and the runner-up gets 300 points. The winner and runner-up of the ATP Tour 250 get 250 points and 150 points, respectively.

Points for rankings can also be accumulated by the players by taking part in the ATP Challenger 125, 110, 100, 90, 80, and 50 tournaments, as well as several levels of lower-ranked ITF events. The ATP Cup, which began in 2020, is a team-based competition between countries, which also gives players the chance to gain points.

The WTA rankings for women's tennis use a similar calculation mechanism to the ATP. The only notable difference is the cap on the number of tournaments. While the ATP uses 'a best of 19' results, the WTA uses 'a best of 16' results for women's Singles and 'a best of 11 results' for Doubles. Points from the 4 Grand Slams and 4 mandatory WTA 1000 tournaments in Indian Wells, Madrid, Miami, and Shanghai have to be included. Apart from these 8 tournaments, 'best other' results from other WTA events are also factored in for points to be accumulated.

TENNIS RANKINGS FOR THE OLYMPICS

From 2000 to 2012, ATP men's Singles ranking points were considered in the Olympics. The WTA ranking was also taken into consideration from 2004. For example, the Olympic gold medallist at London 2012, Andy Murray, earned 750 ATP ranking points while Serena Williams, the women's gold medallist, received 685 WTA ranking points. But this ceased to be effective from the 2016 Rio Olympics. This removal was because of several factors. First, tennis at the Olympics is organized and run by the International Tennis Federation and not by the ATP or WTA.

Second, the lack of substantial prize money at the Olympics makes top players stay away from the event, and the ones that do attend play for their country rather than for individual glory. So, it was decided to do away with individual global rankings in the Olympics, where the emphasis was more on representing one's country than anything else. However, both the ATP and WTA rankings still play a role to determine qualification to the Olympics.

TENNIS AT THE OLYMPICS

A Brief History

Tennis was an integral part of the Olympics and served as an official medal sport from 1896 to 1924. But this early version of tennis was called jeu de paume, and this was an official medal sport at the Olympics in 1908. In 1924, jeu de paume was called real tennis, and there was a demonstration of this form at the 1924 Olympics. Real tennis was played as an indoor, royal court game that featured sloping roofs, walls, and galleries for the spectators. However, the outdoor grass court sport of lawn tennis was also included as a medal event, while its ancestor played a part as a demonstration sport to compare both sports and relive history.

But after the 1924 Summer Games, tennis was removed from the Olympics because of disputes between the International Olympic Committee and the governing body of tennis, the International Lawn Tennis Federation. The two bodies could not come to an agreement about the precise definition of amateur tennis players, and their respective definitions were conflicting. The ILTF failed to enforce its amateur rules at the Olympics, and there were worries that tennis at the Olympics might become so popular that it could overshadow prestigious Grand Slams like Wimbledon. This led to tennis being withdrawn from the Olympics.

Tennis made a comeback to the Olympics several years later, when it was introduced as a demonstration sport at the 1968 and 1984 Olympic Games. However, in Mexico City in 1968, the crowds did not turn up to watch it in large numbers, and there was limited interest in the sport. But it was a different story when tennis was introduced in 1984 at the Los Angeles Olympics as a demonstration sport. This was also the first time the IOC allowed professional athletes to compete in any sports event at the Olympics. Tennis was a huge hit as fans arrived in large numbers, and not a single seat at the venue was unoccupied.

Finally, sense prevailed as the issues of amateur and professional players were resolved with an agreement in 1981 between the ITF and the IOC.

The IOC also changed its policy and allowed professional tennis players to take part in the Olympics. Thus, tennis returned in grand fashion to the Olympics as a full-medal sport at the 1988 Seoul Olympics, held in South Korea. Since then, tennis has been an exciting and prominent feature of the Olympics, and the categories are similar to the Grand Slams, as players compete in men's and women's Singles, men's and women's Doubles, and Mixed Doubles.

AMAZING FACTS ABOUT TENNIS AT THE OLYMPICS

- German legend Steffi Graf won the 'Golden Grand Slam' when she won all four Grand Slams, as well as the Olympic gold medal in 1988 – all in the same calendar year. Only Steffi Graf has managed to achieve this phenomenal feat to date, which makes her a special player for sure.
- However, other tennis players have won a Career Golden Slam, like Andre Agassi, Rafael Nadal, and Novak Djokovic, apart from Steffi Graf, of course. A player achieves a Career Grand Slam when they win all the four Grand Slam tournaments, as well as the Olympic gold medal at some point in their career. But Steffi's achievement stands out as she won everything in a single year.
- The first tennis gold medal in the Olympics was won by John Boland of Ireland. Boland also picked up his second gold medal at the Olympics in Doubles.
- Charlotte 'Chattie' Cooper of England became the first woman to win an individual Olympic event. At

Steffi Graf

the 1900 Paris Olympics, Cooper won the women's tennis Singles and became the first woman in Olympic history to receive a First Place Prize in tennis. This was because medals were given out only from 1904 at the Olympics.

- 1912 was certainly a strange year for tennis, as both the Olympics and Wimbledon were held at the same time. The best tennis players skipped the Olympics to participate at Wimbledon. That was bad tennis timing by the IOC for sure!
- French legend Suzanne Lenglen is considered one of the greatest women tennis players of all time. She won

the Olympic gold medal in 1920. Then, she partnered with Max Decugis to win the gold medal in Mixed Doubles, too. In her third attempt to win the gold, Suzanne failed. She teamed up with Élisabeth d'Ayen for the women's Doubles but had to settle for a bronze medal this time. Well, you can't win them all, even if you are a legend.

- The 1988 Olympics saw tennis return as a medal sport. Miloslav Mečíř of Czechoslovakia won the gold in men's Singles while Steffi Graf won the women's gold.
- The record for the most Olympic gold medals is held by the American Williams sisters, Venus and Serena Williams, with four gold medals apiece.
- The tennis players with the most medals in Olympic history are Venus Williams of America, with four golds and one silver, and British tennis player Kathleen McKane Godfree, with one gold, two silver, and two bronze medals. The two are tied with five medals apiece.
- Scottish player Andy Murray is the only male to have won two Singles golds at the Olympics, as well as defend his title successfully.
- Mixed Doubles made a grand return to the Olympics in London 2012 after a long time in hibernation. The last time it was played at the Olympics as a medal sport was in 1924.
- The Olympic Games in 1896, 1904, 1988, and 1992 awarded bronze medals to both the losing semi-finalists in tennis. After that, a play-off match was held at the Olympics for the bronze medal.
- The Rio Olympics witnessed a strange game of tennis

in the first round, when Australian John Millman beat Lithuania's Ri ardas Berankis 6–0, 6–0. The match was over in just 50 minutes, and this was the first time in Olympic history that a player failed to win a game in a tennis match.

- Tennis was played on clay courts at the Paris 2024 event for the first time since the Barcelona 1992 Olympic Games.
- The most medals in Olympic tennis history have been bagged by Great Britain, with 43 medals, which include 17 gold, 14 silver, and 12 bronze medals. The USA is next on the list with a total of 39 medals.
- But when it comes to gold medals at the Olympics, Team USA has 21 of them, and that's more than any other country.
- Great Britain's Reginald Doherty has the most individual gold medals in men's tennis at the Olympics. He has won three gold medals.
- Wheelchair tennis is an event at the Olympics. There are two different wheelchair tennis categories. The first is 'Open', for athletes with lower limb impairment. The second is 'Quad', for those with both upper limb and lower limb impairment.

THE DAVIS CUP

The Davis Cup is the top draw in terms of an international team event in tennis. The players represent their nation as they do in the Olympics, and over the years, the Davis Cup has earned a reputation that is similar to the football World Cup. Run by the International Tennis Federation, this annual contest witnesses different countries competing for top honours in tennis in a knockout format.

A Brief History

Originally known as the International Lawn Tennis Challenge, the Davis Cup was first played in 1900. In fact, it was the brainchild of Dwight Filley Davis, the captain of the first American tennis team. He thought of starting a challenge tennis match between the USA and Great Britain. Because of a lack of funds, Davis bought the trophy with his own money and set the ball rolling. Hence, the Davis Cup is rightly named after him. Davis also became the first president of the American Tennis Federation. The first Davis Cup match was held in Boston, with Longwood Cricket Club serving as the venue. Yes, the Americans also played cricket then. The Brits had a stronger team, but the Americans shocked them and won the first Davis Cup, which had only two nations competing in its inaugural event. Dwight Davis was part of the winning American team. 1905 witnessed the expansion of the Davis Cup, when teams from France, Austria, Belgium, and a combined team of Australia and New Zealand joined in. The defending champion of the Davis Cup had it rather easy as they would proceed straight to the finals in the next tournament without having to play a single match. Then, they would sit in the sun and wait for the best team to emerge from the other teams, whom they would play in the final. This made defending the Davis Cup title easier than in the present times.

In 1907, Australasia, the combined team from Australia

and New Zealand, won the Davis Cup, and this was the first time that Britain or the USA did not lift the title. In the 1950s and 1960s, Australia had some really talented players, like Rod Laver, Margaret Court, Evonne Goolagong Cawley, John Newcombe, and Ken Rosewall. It was considered the golden age of Australian tennis, and no wonder that Australia dominated the Davis Cup, winning it 15 times from 1950 to 1967.

The Davis Cup became a knockout tournament in 1972 to manage time and scheduling. Now, zone champions had to compete against each other for a spot in the final. However, only amateurs could participate in the Davis Cup, according to the tournament rules, and it was not until 1973 that professional tennis players were allowed to participate. Until 1973, only four nations had won the Davis Cup: Great Britain, the United States, Australia, and France. But in 1974, none of these nations managed to reach the final, in another first. South Africa and India reached the finals instead. Sadly, India forfeited the match and refused to travel to South Africa to play the Davis Cup final there as a protest against apartheid. South Africa won the Davis Cup without playing the final and became the fifth nation to do so. 1975 witnessed an underdog final at the Davis Cup as Sweden beat Czechoslovakia to become the sixth nation to win the Davis Cup.

The Davis Cup Format

In the 1980s, further changes were made to the Davis Cup format. The 16 best national teams were placed in a world group, while the other national teams were divided according to geographical zones.

In 1989, the tiebreak was introduced in the Davis Cup. Better late than never! 2022 saw a new record in terms of Davis Cup participation, as 148 countries entered the tournament for team supremacy in tennis. However, not all those nations managed to take part in the final round of the Davis Cup. The format of the Davis Cup needs a detailed explanation for an understanding of the same.

A 'tie' is an elimination round, while a 'rubber' refers to an individual match. Each tie consists of five rubbers. The nation that wins three or more of the five rubbers, four Singles, and one Doubles match is declared the winner. While there are home and away ties for qualification to the Davis Cup, the finals are based on a knockout system. Eight teams play the Final 8 Round, including the host nation. The host nation is given a spot in the Final 8 only if it matches the following criteria:

- The host nation must be ranked in the Top 50 nations in the Davis Cup rankings

or

- One of the players of the host nation must have an individual ranking in the Top 10.

If these criteria are not met, the eighth spot in the Final 8 is reallocated to another country as a wild card entry. Matches in the Final 8, however, are best-of-three sets, with 2 Singles ties and 1 Doubles tie. The team needs to win 2 matches now instead of 3.

The Davis Cup Trophy

The original Davis Cup trophy was a silver salad bowl. This was probably because Dwight Filley Davis used his own money for the same. Today, thanks to the expansion process over the years, new mahogany plinths have been added to the base of the trophy, where the names of the champions have been continuously engraved. Today, this beautiful trophy features 217 ounces of silver and is 110 cm tall with a diameter of 107 cm. It weighs 231.5 pounds.

Davis Cup Trophy

A firm of silversmiths named Shreve, Crump & Low of Boston, Massachusetts, made the first trophy with the famous bowl donated by Davis in 1900. This bowl was designed by William Durgin and crafted by Rowland Rhodes and is made of sterling silver with the interior burnished in gold. In 1921, a silver tray called 'The Salver' was added by Black, Starr & Frost of New York.

AMAZING FACTS ABOUT THE DAVIS CUP

- The most successful team in the Davis Cup is the USA, with 32 titles. The USA has also been the runner-up as many as 29 times. Australia is a close second, with an impressive 28 titles. Britain and France have won 10 titles apiece.
- The most successful player in the Davis Cup is undoubtedly Roy Emerson, the legend from Australia. Emerson helped Australia win eight Davis Cup titles.
- The most successful captain in the Davis Cup is also an Australian. Harry Hopman was the captain of 16 victorious teams of Australia.
- There are four instances when the Davis Cup was not held. The outbreak of World War I saw no tennis action from 1915 to 1918, and the tournament was again suspended from 1940 to 1945 because of World War II. In 2020, the Davis Cup did not take place because of the Covid-19 pandemic. But it was not held in 1910 for an interesting reason. In 1909, Australasia, a combined team of Australia and New Zealand, won the Davis Cup title. The rules at the time demanded that a country must issue a challenge to the defending champions for the tournament to take place. But no one challenged Australasia, and as a result, there was no tournament in 1910.
- The Davis Cup has become fiercely competitive today. The last time the USA won the title was way back in 2007. Great Britain last won it in 2015 and had to wait for 76 long years before that to win it. Australia has been waiting to lift the Davis Cup for two decades now.

- In 2022, Canada won the Davis Cup to join the increasing list of first-time winners like South Africa, Argentina, Italy, Serbia, and Switzerland.
- Only India and Romania have played more than one final of the Davis Cup without being crowned the champion. India was runner-up on as many as three occasions, in 1966, 1974, and 1987. Indian tennis fans are hopeful that the jinx will be broken someday.
- Indian tennis player Leander Paes is one of the most successful Doubles players in tennis history and has also won an Olympic bronze at the Olympics. He has represented India at the Davis Cup for 30 long years.
- Former Italian tennis player Nicola Pietrangeli has played the most individual matches at the Davis Cup. The Italian played as many as 164 Davis Cup matches for Italy and won 120 of those matches. Even this is a record! But sadly, Nicola Pietrangeli could never win the Davis Cup for Italy, even though he won the French Open twice.
- The record for the longest winning streak in the Davis Cup Singles ties is held by Marcos Baghdatis of Cyprus. He won 36 Singles matches in a row.
- San Marino is a tiny country in Europe and has one of the weakest tennis teams at the Davis Cup. But San Marino tennis players hold some interesting records at the tournament, even though they haven't made a mark at the Davis Cup. The youngest and oldest tennis player to play the Davis Cup both belong to San Marino. In 2011, Marco de Rossi made his Davis Cup debut when he was just 13 years and 319 days old. This record will never be broken as the current

rules don't allow players under 14 to play the Davis Cup. Vittorio Pellandra, at 66 years and 104 days, became the oldest player to participate in the Davis Cup when he played for San Marino. That's a tough one to beat, too!

- The official fastest serve in tennis history was recorded by the ATP at the 2016 Davis Cup. American John Isner fired a serve that travelled like a bullet at 253 km/h as the USA played Australia in a Davis Cup tie. This was a new world record.
- The Billie Jean King Cup, which was formerly called the Fed Cup, is the women's version of the Davis Cup. The Fed Cup was founded in 1963 to celebrate the 50th anniversary of the ITF. The trophy was renamed after the American tennis legend Billie Jean King.

8

GOATS, LEGENDS, AND GREATS OF TENNIS

Tennis has produced many superstars over the years. All of us have a personal favourite whom we've idolized as a child or while growing up. Many of these GOATs, legends, and greats of tennis have received the ultimate recognition for their contributions and achievements by being inducted into the Tennis Hall of Fame. Let's take a look at some of these impressive performers and their stats in men's and women's Singles.

A FEW GOOD MEN: TOP 20 MALE PLAYERS IN TENNIS HISTORY

Bill Tilden

Tennis legend Bill Tilden was the first American who won Wimbledon in 1920, paving the way for others. He won a total of 10 Grand Slams, including a joint-record 7 US Championships titles. He is also rumoured to have the second-fastest serve in tennis history.

René Lacoste

Jean René Lacoste was one of the greatest French tennis players, who became the best player in the world from 1926 to 1927. Lacoste won 7 Grand Slam titles, making a name for himself as a legend. He also earned the famous nickname of 'Crocodile', thanks to his business acumen, by creating the famous Lacoste tennis shirt in 1929.

René Lacoste

Rod Laver

Australian Rodney George Laver or Rod Laver is right up there among the greatest players in tennis history.

Rod picked up the sport early on as his mother was a professional tennis player. Nicknamed 'The Rocket' by his Davis Cup team captain, Rod Laver dominated his opponents with his aggression and agility. He won a total of 228 career titles, which included 20 Grand Slam titles in both Singles and Doubles. Rod Laver reached the final of 14 Grand Slams in men's Singles and won 11 of them, which was a record then. Rod also won the Grand Prix twice, which means winning all four major titles in a year. He achieved this in 1962 and 1969. Rod Laver was World No. 1 for seven years! Definitely a GOAT!

Rod Laver

Roy Emerson

Australian tennis legend Roy Emerson won 12 Grand Slam titles, a record that stood for 33 years. He's also among the nine legends to achieve a Career Grand Slam. The others are Don Budge, Rod Laver, Fred Perry, Roy Emerson, Andre Agassi, Roger Federer, Rafael Nadal, Novak Djokovic, and Carlos Alcaraz.

Fred Perry

British tennis legend Fred Perry became the world champion in table tennis when he was just 20 years old. He then decided to play tennis and create history. Perry became the only English player to have won all four Grand Slam titles and also the first man to achieve the Career Grand Slam. He won 8 Grand Slam Singles titles and 6 Doubles titles.

Don Budge

American tennis legend Don Budge was the second man to achieve the Career Grand Slam after Fred Perry. But he is the first tennis player to win all the Grand Slams in a single year, a feat called Calendar Grand Slam, in 1938. Budge won 6 Grand Slam Singles titles and 4 Grand Slam Doubles titles in his illustrious career.

Björn Borg

Swedish legend Björn Borg's off-court lifestyle, good looks, and playing ability won him many fans and drew large crowds. Björn Borg won 64 career titles, which include 11 Grand Slams, as he won Wimbledon and the French Open for three consecutive years. His Grand Slam Singles win record is 41%, and he has won 90% of those matches. He's also won 3 Grand Slam titles without losing a single set. But his failure to win the US Open and the Australian Open makes him fall short of the GOAT status.

John Mcenroe

John McEnroe was born in West Germany and raised in New York, USA, where he began playing tennis as an eight-year-old. He was a passionate and talented tennis player, renowned for his versatile play, as well as for his temper tantrums. He won 7 Grand Slam Singles titles, 9 men's Doubles titles, and 1 Mixed Doubles title. His inability to win the Singles title at the French Open and the Australian Open makes him a legend of the game rather than a GOAT.

Jimmy Connors

American tennis legend Jimmy Connors was a fierce competitor who played left-handed. In 1974, Connors was ranked World No. 1 but was notorious for his bad behaviour on court. Despite being a great player, he was also aggressive and the most rebellious player in tennis history. Connors won 10 Grand Slam titles, out of which 8 came in men's Singles. His resume just falls short of being one of the greatest because he never won the French Open.

Ivan Lendl

Ivan Lendl was a major force in tennis during the 1980s and put the Czech Republic on the tennis map. This tennis legend was one of the best players in his era on all surfaces and held the No. 1 spot for several years in his prime. He won 8 Grand Slam Singles titles, and only the Wimbledon title famously eluded this champion tennis player. He reached the Wimbledon final twice, in 1986 and 1987, but lost to Boris Becker and Pat Cash, respectively. Lendl has reached the semi-finals of Wimbledon seven times and is considered by many to be the best grass-court player who has never won Wimbledon.

Stefan Edberg

Swedish legend Stefan Edberg was famous for his serve and volley game. His backhand volley was especially spectacular. Edberg was ranked World No. 1 in both men's Singles and Doubles, a feat matched only by John McEnroe in the Open Era. Edberg won 6 Singles Grand Slam titles and 3 Grand Slam titles in men's Doubles. Stefan Edberg was the first and only player to win a junior Grand Slam. But he couldn't replicate his success by winning a Career Grand Slam in his professional career. Edberg is one of the few players to reach the final of all four Grand Slam tournaments. He managed to win 3 Grand Slams but lost in the final of the French Open in 1989 to a 17-year-old Michael Chang., Post retirement, Edberg coached Roger Federer from January 2014 to December 2015.

Mats Wilander

Mats Wilander is another Swedish legend. He was the first winner of three Grand Slams in a single year in 1988 since Jimmy Connors did it in 1974. After winning the Australian Open, French Open, and the US Open, Wilander discovered he was World No. 1. But his dream of a Career Grand

Slam ended at Wimbledon as he lost in the quarter-finals. Mats Wilander has won 7 Grand Slam Singles titles and 7 Doubles titles as well.

Boris Becker

John McEnroe was the youngest man to reach the semi-finals of a Grand Slam until German legend Boris Becker arrived on the scene to break this record. A 17-year-old Boris Becker became the youngest to win a Grand Slam at Wimbledon in 1985. He is considered the pioneer of the power game by many because of his booming serve and

Boris Becker

all-court game. Out of the 64 titles Becker has won, there are 6 Grand Slam Singles victories. He has won all the Grand Slams, except the French Open. Today, although Martina Hingis is the youngest Grand Slam champion in tennis history and Michael Chang is the youngest man to win a Grand Slam, Boris Becker remains the youngest man to win Wimbledon.

Pete Sampras

Pete Sampras became an icon in the United States and worldwide with his superlative tennis performances. Big Pete was the first to use his powerful serve as a weapon and utilize his attacking game to completely dominate his opponents. His 14 Grand Slam Singles titles were a record when he retired in 2002. This record stood till 2009, when Roger Federer broke it. Even though he never won the French Open, Pete Sampras was the GOAT of men's tennis during his playing days. It was only after he retired that a trio of superstars outshone his record to become the Big Three in tennis.

Jim Courier

American Jim Courier was one of the tennis greats, and it was especially tough for him as he was pitted against some of the biggest names in his era, like Swede Stefan Edberg and fellow Americans Pete Sampras, Andre Agassi, and Michael Chang. This was called the 'Golden Age of American tennis', and Courier was a key member of the mix. The fighter that he was, Courier managed to reach the finals of all four Grand Slams, becoming the youngest player in tennis history, at 22, to achieve the feat. His aggressive baseline game and amazing levels of fitness helped Courier win 4 Grand Slam titles in his career, including the French Open and the Australian Open, both of which he won twice.

Jim Courier

Andre Agassi

Andre Agassi brought flamboyance into men's tennis, and his natural talent on the court, combined with his tenacity, made him a legend of the game. A big part of 'The Golden age of American tennis', his 21-year-long career was full of ups and downs. He has won 8 Grand Slam Singles titles. But Agassi has won all the Grand Slams in his career, as well as an Olympic gold medal, making him the first male tennis player to complete a Career Golden Slam. The others to achieve this phenomenal feat are Agassi's wife, Steffi Graf, Serena Williams, Rafael Nadal, and Novak Djokovic.

Andre Agassi

THE BIG THREE

Roger Federer

Switzerland found its sports icon when Roger Federer burst on the scene and dominated the sport between the Pete Sampras and the Novak Djokovic era. Federer is also among the three male tennis players to win all four

Grand Slam Singles titles and the year-end championship in their career. The other two are Andre Agassi and Novak Djokovic. Federer has won an astonishing 20 Grand Slam titles, making him a tennis GOAT. He reigned as World No. 1 for a record 310 weeks, and many consider him the greatest tennis player of all time.

Roger Federer

Rafael Nadal

Rafael Nadal is Spain's first tennis superstar. The 2000s saw the best rivalry in men's tennis and the dawn of a new era, with Nadal, Federer, and Djokovic fighting for top tennis honours. They are known as the 'Big Three' of tennis and are arguably the greatest the game has ever seen if you consider their accomplishments and titles. Nadal has won the second-most Grand Slam Singles titles, with

22. He has also won all the Grand Slams, as well as the Olympic gold. But the only thing that puts Federer and Djokovic ahead of the Spaniard is that Nadal won 14 of his 22 Grand Slam titles at the French Open as he was simply unstoppable and unbeatable on clay.

Rafael Nadal

Novak Djokovic

Serbian Novak Djokovic has won the most Grand Slam titles in tennis history. He has 24 men's Singles titles, which makes Sampras's 14 titles seem insignificant. Djokovic has won all the Grand Slam titles and is still going strong on the tennis court, even as the other two in the 'Big Three' have retired from professional tennis. Like Nadal at the French

Open, Djokovic found greater success at the Australian Open, where he won a record 10 titles, the most by any player. He also won the Olympic gold in Paris in 2024 to complete the elusive Career Golden Slam, a feat that only he and Nadal have achieved among the 'Big Three', as Federer hasn't won an Olympic gold medal. That's what puts Novak slightly above in terms of stats when you compare him to his biggest tennis rivals.

Novak Djokovic

Andy Murray

Tennis great Andy Murray won 3 Grand Slams and 2 Olympic gold medals in his career, which is commendable in an era when the 'Big Three' were in supreme form. He was also the first British player to win Wimbledon after Fred Perry, ending a 77-year drought. Perhaps that's why the British media have coined the term 'The Big Four', including Andy Murray in the 'Big Three'.

TOP 10 BEST MALE PLAYERS IN TENNIS HISTORY

Creating a list of the Top 10 male players in tennis history is a cumbersome task. So many factors have to be weighed in, such as the difference in playing conditions in various eras, the changes in fitness levels, and the availability of tennis equipment, for starters. Despite the challenges, this needed to be done as 'TOP 10' lists are in vogue today. This list is based on several factors, like the number of Grand Slams won, style of play, ability to play on different surfaces, and the playing level of opponents faced. The players who have played tennis in eras that have been highly competitive have been preferred over others.

Position	Name	Nationality	Grand Slams Won
1	Novak Djokovic	Serbia	24
2	Roger Federer	Switzerland	20
3	Rafael Nadal	Spain	22
4	Pete Sampras	USA	14
5	Rod Laver	Australia	11
6	Björn Borg	Sweden	11
7	John McEnroe	USA	7
8	Ivan Lendl	Czech	8
9	Jimmy Connors	USA	8
10	Andre Agassi	USA	8

THE IRON LADIES OF TENNIS: TOP 10 GREATEST PLAYERS

No. 10: Evonne Goolagong/Martina Hingis

Two great women are tied at the tenth position in our exclusive list. They are Swiss tennis player Martina Hingis and Australian tennis player Evonne Goolagong.

Australian great Goolagong often escapes our attention because she was overshadowed by her more illustrious rivals, like Chris Evert and Martina Navratilova. But

Evonne Goolagong

despite such competitiveness in women's tennis during her era, Goolagong won 7 Grand Slam titles and was ranked No. 1 in the world in 1976. The only Grand Slam Evonne Goolagong failed to win was the US Open, and she was extremely unlucky not to complete a Career Grand Slam as she reached the finals of the US Open four times in a row from 1973 to 1976. Goolagong also holds a unique record: She was the only mother since World War I to have won the Wimbledon title, having achieved this feat in 1980 after she had given birth to her daughter three years earlier.

Martina Hingis won 5 Grand Slam Singles titles, and only the French Open eluded her. She is a strong contender

Martina Hingis

for this list as she was ranked No. 1 in the world for 209 weeks. She also has as many as 13 Grand Slam Doubles titles and 7 Mixed Doubles titles, making her a complete tennis player. Hingis became famous for being the youngest player to win a Grand Slam as she was only 15 years and 9 months old when she won the Wimbledon Doubles title in 1996, partnering with Helena Sukova. Prior to this, Hingis was also the youngest player to win the junior Grand Slam in 1993 when she was 12 years old. It's quite a shame that her career was short-lived and that her first retirement happened when she was just 23 years old. Because of her injuries, Hingis had to restrict her career to Doubles and shone there as well. If she'd had a longer career, Martina Hingis would have definitely won more Grand Slams and been somewhere close to the top of this list for sure.

No. 9: Justine Henin

Belgian Justine Henin was a powerful player and tremendously athletic despite her small stature. Henin's powerful serve and volley game and baseline play on clay surfaces were equally impressive. In 2003, Henin became the world No. 1 by winning both the French Open and the US Open. In 2004, she won the Olympic Gold medal, along with an Australian Open title. Despite winning 7 Grand Slams in her career, Henin could not win the Wimbledon title, thus denying her a Golden Grand Slam after more than 20 years of competitive professional tennis.

No. 8: Venus Williams

The lesser famous of the Williams sisters is No. 8 on the list of the best women players in tennis history. Too bad Venus Williams had to compete with her supremely talented younger sister, Serena. Otherwise, Venus could have had more than her 7 Grand Slam titles. Consider the fact that the most famous sisters in tennis have faced off nine times in a Grand Slam final, with Serena emerging victorious seven times. Also, Venus's career was plagued by injuries, which denied her a place higher on this list. Venus was in top form in the 2000s, and four of her 7 Grand Slam wins came during the period between 2000 and 2001. She was exceptional at Wimbledon, winning 5 titles. She also won the gold medal at the Sydney Olympics, but the French Open and the Australian Open were Grand Slams she never won.

Venus Williams

No. 7: Billie Jean King

The queen of tennis during her era, as well as the queen of Wimbledon, American Billie Jean King was a tennis powerhouse. She dominated women's tennis from the mid-1960s to the mid-1970s. She won an astonishing 39 Grand Slam titles, which included 12 Singles titles, 16 women's Doubles titles, and 11 Mixed Doubles titles. 32 of her 39 Grand Slam victories came between 1966 and 1975, which was the peak of her professional tennis career. In 1972, Billie Jean King won the French Open, a title that had eluded her for many years. This completed her Career Grand Slam, and she became one of just five women at that time who had achieved this.

1972 also saw the emergence of Chris Evert as a challenger to King's throne. Their rivalry was characterized by a sharp contrast in playing styles. King was famous for her attacking play, while Evert played a cool baseline game. King dominated on grass and carpet, while Evert won on clay and hard courts. Even though Evert was clearly the new queen of tennis now, Billie Jean King still dominated the grass courts of Wimbledon from 1966 to 1975, lifting the title six times. Women's tennis owes a huge debt to the great Billie Jean King, who threatened to boycott the 1973 US Open along with others until women players were given equal prize money as men. This push led to the US Open becoming the first Grand Slam to offer equal pay for men and women, and the other Grand Slams followed suit in time. Billie Jean King was an advocate of women's rights, gender equality, and social justice. Who can forget her bizarre and historic 'Battle of the Sexes' tennis match against Bobby Riggs, who had challenged her? King accepted the challenge and defeated Riggs in quick time. Billie Jean King demonstrated that whatever he thought only men could do, women could do at par if not better. Being a lesbian, Billie Jean King also fought for LGBTQ+ rights during her playing days.

No. 6: Monica Seles

Born in Yugoslavia, Monica Seles played tennis for the United States. She dominated women's tennis from 1990 to 1992, winning 7 of her 9 Grand Slam titles during this period. She dethroned Steffi Graf to become the top-ranked

Monica Seles

woman tennis player in the world in 1991. Her battles with Steffi Graf were classics, and they played a total of 16 matches, in which Graf won ten times and Seles won six times. Tennis fans were denied of more such classic encounters because of an unfortunate incident in 1993. Monica Seles was attacked and stabbed by a crazy fan while she was on the court. The attack traumatized Seles and forced her to take a break from the sport. She was never the same when she made a comeback after two years, and it was clear that the incident had affected and upset her greatly. Case in point that her best years were before that stabbing incident is that Monica Seles had won three of the four matches she played against Graf when she was between 17 and 19 years old. After her comeback, Seles managed to defeat Graf only once, but great player that she was, Monica Seles won the Australian Open in 1996. This was her sole post-attack Grand Slam victory, though, and she would have certainly won more if not for that deranged idiot who stabbed her. Monica Seles played professional tennis till 2003 and announced her official retirement in 2008.

No. 5: Chris Evert

Chris Evert dominated women's tennis from the mid-1970s to the early 1980s. Her baseline play had the precision of a machine, and her two-handed backhand shot was the weapon in her arsenal. Chris Evert holds the record of reaching the most Grand Slam Singles finals as she did so 34 times. She won 18 of those finals and every Grand Slam at least twice. If that's not enough achievement, to be at No. 5 on this list, she was No. 1 in the world for as long as seven years, with a win percentage in Singles of more than 90%. Evert's brilliance is magnified considering the legendary rivalries with Billie Jean King early on in her career and the one with Martina Navratilova later. The rivalry between Chris Evert and Martina Navratilova was legendary and lasted from the 1970s to the 1980s. The two played each other 80 times, which included 60 finals. Although the head-to-head record stands 43–37 in favour of Navratilova, Evert was more dominant on clay, while Navratilova excelled on grass. Also, Evert was two years older than Navratilova, so it was Even-Stevens to be fair. But thanks to this rivalry, women's tennis only became more popular. The fierce rivalry slowly developed into a deep, lifelong friendship. That's the beauty of tennis!

No. 4: Margaret Court

Many old-timers and tennis experts are of the opinion that Australian legend Margaret Court is the best women's tennis player of all time. There's logic in that argument as Margaret Court has a Grand Slam record that players dream to achieve. She has won a total of 64 Grand Slams. If that sounds unbelievable, the break-up is mind-boggling – 24 Grand Slam Singles titles, 19 women's Doubles titles, and 21 Mixed Doubles titles. She's the only player in tennis history who has won multiple Grand Slams in all the playing categories at all four major tournaments. In fact, Slovak Daniela Hantuchová is the only other woman to win a Grand Slam in Mixed Doubles, but Margaret Court did this twice. Court was the best player in women's tennis from the 1960s to the early 1970s and the first woman to feature weights and fitness training in her regimen for a lengthy career that was injury free. But we still have Margaret Court at No. 4 on the list despite her stellar achievements. Read on to know more.

Margaret Court

No. 3: Martina Navratilova

Our No. 3 is the tennis icon Martina Navratilova, who was born to play the game. This tough lady dominated the scene in women's tennis from the late 1970s to the mid-1980s. Thanks to her, the big serve and volley game returned to women's tennis. Martina Navratilova has won 59 Grand Slam titles compared to Margaret Court's 64 titles. This includes 18 Grand Slam Singles titles, 31 women's Doubles titles, and 10 Mixed Doubles titles. But the reason we've put her ahead of Court is that Martina Navratilova won a mind-blowing 395 professional titles in Singles and Doubles over an extraordinary career that spanned 22 years. Also, other factors like key rivalries and the quality of opposition tilted the balance in Navratilova's favour. With stats like that, it's actually tragic that she's No. 3 on this special list.

No. 2: Steffi Graf

The most wonderful thing about sport, and tennis in particular, is that a legend always replaces another one. That's what has made tennis such a fascinating sport over the years. In 1986, a German named Steffi Graf announced her arrival on the women's tennis scene after a shock victory over Chris Evert. Steffi Graf slowly became the undisputed No. 1 in women's tennis, as well as every schoolboy's fantasy. Steffi's ability to play equally well on all surfaces endeared her to fans globally. She maintained this consistency throughout her 17-year career, which is remarkable, just like being ranked No. 1 in the world for a record 377 weeks. This is unmatched by any player, male or female. Steffi won 22 Grand Slam Singles titles and also won all the Grand Slams to complete her Career Grand Slam. Her amazing feat of winning all the Grand Slams, as well as the Olympic gold in the same year, made her achieve the 'Calendar Golden Grand Slam'. Steffi Graf is the only player in tennis history to have achieved this feat.

Steffi Graf ruled women's tennis from the late 1980s to the mid-1990s. She retired in 1999, and guess what her ranking was? No. 3 in the world! Greatest women's tennis player in the world, you say? We would love to agree, but

Steffi is No. 2 on the list. We know we are upsetting many fans, including oldies who were schoolboy fans of Steffi once upon a time. But as said earlier, the beauty of tennis is that one legend is replaced by another.

No. 1: Serena Williams

Serena Williams is numero uno on our list simply because of the longevity of her career and the way she dominated all her rivals with her great strength and impressive talent. It's tough to choose between Graf and Williams as the greatest player in tennis history as both dominated

Serena Williams

their respective eras. But Serena has the slightest of edges because of her high level of tennis over such a long career merged with the impressive record of 23–10 in all Grand Slam Singles finals. Serena's career has certainly been an impressive one, with 23 Grand Slam Singles titles, which is the most won in the Open Era, and the second-most of all time. Serena is the only tennis player to achieve a Career Golden Slam in both Singles and Doubles and has also won 73 WTA Tour-level Singles titles. Add to that 14 Grand Slams Doubles titles, which she won by teaming up with elder sister Venus Williams. This duo was unbeaten in Grand Slam finals, which is another record. Also add 4 Olympic gold medals, one in women's Singles and three in women's Doubles.

As avid tennis fans, we await the legend who will replace Serena Williams in women's tennis.

A Grand Celebration of Serena Williams | All 23 Grand Slam Titles

9

AMAZING FACTS ABOUT WOMEN'S TENNIS

A BRIEF HISTORY OF WOMEN'S TENNIS

The Victorians in England were the first in the world to encourage women's tennis. But the Victorian women who played tennis in the early days were dressed rather differently from the tennis players that we see today. Prudish Victorian society demanded that women tennis players cover their arms completely while playing. Their ankles were also not supposed to be visible, and they had to wear gowns that almost touched the ground. Whoever made these costume rules had to be daft, as a woman also had to wear three starched petticoats under all that clothing to make the dress blossom out according to Victorian tennis fashion. No wonder there were few tennis players during Victorian times. Imagine wearing such a costumed monstrosity to play tennis in the heat! Anyone for tennis? No, thank you! I'd rather stay indoors and read a book.

If that wasn't enough, the notoriously painful Victorian corset was also mandatory on court to maintain an hourglass figure for the viewing pleasure of the spectators. This ensemble was also rather expensive, which restricted Victorian tennis only to the rich and privileged. Add to the cumbersome sporting attire heeled boots, a stiff whalebone collar, and a wide-brimmed hat. Sounds more like tea-party wear than tennis clothing. It's similar to playing football dressed in a suit. It must have been quite a battle running to the net to return those drop shots or running back to the baseline to return a lob without tripping on your gown and falling flat on your hat or face. Imagine someone like Maria Sharapova playing in Victorian clothing or a Victorian tennis player wearing Sharapova's cool outfit. That would have been quite a sight!

But we must thank the Victorians. It is thanks to their efforts to promote women's tennis that the Wimbledon Championships, the oldest tennis tournament in the world, added ladies Singles to their schedule in 1884. The Irish will be mighty proud as they are when they beat the English in something. That's because the Irish Championships included women's tennis in 1879, thus prompting Wimbledon in England to follow suit.

But can you imagine a world without women's tennis? It would indeed be so boring and listless. Women's tennis was an integral part of growing up in the pre-internet era, where every boy and girl of the 1980s and 1990s would have posters of Steffi Graf, Gabriela Sabatini, and Martina Navratilova, among others, torn from sports magazines and stuck on doors and bedroom walls. How boring modern tennis would be without the serve and volley game of Martina Navratilova, the elegant baseline play of Chris Evert, the magnificent moves of Steffi Graf, the power-packed Williams sisters, the famous grunts of Monica Seles, and of course, the bold and the beautiful talent of Maria Sharapova.

WTA PLAYER IN FOCUS: AMAZING FACTS ABOUT MARIA SHARAPOVA

Famous Russian tennis player Maria Sharapova is the perfect combination of beauty and talent in women's tennis. Famously known as Masha in tennis circles, her journey from a childhood of hardships to become a successful tennis player and one of the most successful women is an inspirational one for all young girls and women.

Maria Sharapova moved from Russia to the USA as a seven-year-old, accompanied by her father, with only $700 in her pocket, to become the highest-paid female athlete for a decade. What's more, she could not speak English when she moved to America.

A young Masha's raw talent was spotted early on by tennis legend Martina Navratilova, and this led to her being coached professionally at the IMG Academy. Sharapova did not prove Navratilova wrong and became the youngest girl in tennis history to reach the final of the Australian Open Junior Championship. She also reached the Wimbledon final in the same year, in 2002.

Sharapova's meteoric rise to superstardom in women's tennis is nothing short of a fairy tale. Maria Sharapova became the only Russian tennis player to achieve the Career Grand Slam by winning all four Grand Slam titles. She did this when she was just 21 years old and is 1 of the 10 women in professional tennis to achieve this feat.

- In 1997, Maria Sharapova signed a lucrative deal with Nike when she was only 11 years old. Since then, Nike has been her biggest sponsor. In 2010, Nike signed another deal with Sharapova, which was to last for eight years and was worth $70 million. This was a historic deal made with a female athlete then. From $700 to $70 million is dream stuff, really. Tennis makes dreams come true!
- In 2015, *Forbes* listed Maria Sharapova as the richest female athlete in the world, with earnings of $29.7 million. Tennis earnings were a small part of this astronomical sum as Masha made about $23 million through her high-profile endorsements alone.
- In 2004, Sharapova became the third youngest woman to win Wimbledon at the age of 17 years and 75 days. This victory fetched her global stardom as she defeated Serena Williams in straight sets in the final. Sharapova became the first Russian to clinch the Wimbledon title and the fourth Russian in tennis history to win a Grand Slam.
- Maria Sharapova stands at a towering 6 feet 2 inches and is the third-tallest player of all time in women's tennis. That's the same height as the GOAT of men's tennis, Novak Djokovic. She also scaled new heights in tennis as she was ranked World No. 1 by the WTA five times, for 21 weeks in total.
- Inspired by the success of her modelling career, Sharapova displayed her growing business acumen

by launching her own candy company, aptly named Sugarpova.

- Maria Sharapova's tennis career ended a bit strangely. In 2020, she announced her retirement from tennis through an essay that was published in *Vanity Fair* and *Vogue*, instead of opting for a press conference, which is the traditional route taken by tennis players. But Sharapova plays by her own rules.
- In 2025, Maria Sharapova was inducted into the International Tennis Hall of Fame.

Maria Sharapova

SOME SMASHING FACTS

- In 1874, a woman named Mary Ewing Outerbridge introduced lawn tennis to the United States of America.
- Before 1903, women played tennis from the baseline, without much on-court movement. The one to change this boring game was an American woman named Hazel Hotchkiss Wightman, who is also known as the 'Queen Mother of Tennis'. Wightman set things right in 1903 in San Francisco, California, by introducing net play and the volley, thus transforming women's tennis.
- The first American woman to win the Wimbledon title was May Sutton Bundy. She won in 1904 and repeated her success in 1907. But Bundy played her most memorable match at the US Open in Forest Hills in 1930, even though she lost the match. Bundy fractured her leg, but instead of quitting like most players would have done today, unbelievably, she played the rest of the match using a crutch as support. Hope she did not use it to smash the tennis ball. Bundy might have lost that match, but she certainly won many hearts.
- In the context of tennis, 'breaking the sound barrier' does not refer to anything in tennis at all. It actually refers to a fighter jet flying overhead at supersonic speed as a tennis match is in progress. This causes a sonic boom that stops play and unsettles players and spectators alike. This has been observed at the French Open.
- African American tennis player Althea Gibson broke the race barrier in tennis by becoming the first African

American to play at the US Open in 1950. Althea tasted Grand Slam success from 1956 to 1958 by winning as many as 11 Grand Slam titles. These included 5 Grand Slam Singles titles.

- The first woman to complete the Grand Slam of tennis by winning all four Grand Slams in a single year was American tennis player Maureen Connolly. She achieved this incredible feat in 1953. The two other women who have achieved this amazing feat are Australian Margaret Court in 1970 and German Steffi Graf in 1988.
- Lady Meherbai Tata, wife of Sir Dorabji Tata, was the first Indian woman to play tennis at the Olympics. She played Mixed Doubles at the Paris 1924 Games by partnering with M. Saleem. She famously wore a traditional Parsi sari as she played, probably raising even those Victorian eyebrows. But it was a proud moment for India as Lady Meherbai Tata represented her cultural heritage.
- The winner of the most Singles titles in tennis history is Martina Navratilova. She won a staggering 167 titles. Both Martina Navratilova and Steffi Graf have earned more than $20 million over their stellar careers.
- Martina Navratilova held the record for being the oldest woman to win a Grand Slam in the Open Era. She won Wimbledon in 1990, when she was 33 years old. This record was broken by Serena Williams in 2017, when she won the Australian Open aged 35 years and 124 days. Serena is the only woman who has won a Grand Slam Singles title after turning 35. That's career longevity and success for you!

- The first tournament exclusively for women professional tennis players was the 1970 Virginia Slims Tennis Tournament. Tennis icon Billie Jean King was one of the organizers. The very next year, she became the first female athlete in sports to earn in excess of $100,000 in a single season.

THE BATTLE OF THE SEXES

1973 witnessed a strange tennis match that was labelled the 'Battle of the Sexes'. This was an exhibition match played between former men's champion Bobby Riggs and top-ranked female tennis player Billie Jean King. The match was highly publicized and gave a much-needed boost to women's tennis.

The Background

The premise for the 'Battle of the Sexes' was laid in the same year as Bobby Riggs played women's tennis legend and World No. 2 Margaret Court in a similar match. The 55-year old Riggs won this match, thrashing Margaret Court in straight sets 6–1, 6–2. This prequel to the 'Battle of the Sexes' was famously known as 'Mother's Day Massacre' and was intended to prove that men were superior to women in tennis. Riggs also wanted to justify his personal crusade that there was no way that equal pay should exist for men and women in tennis.

The Challenge

To cement his point, Bobby Riggs challenged World No. 1 Billie Jean King a few months later. Incidentally, Bobby

Riggs was regarded as one of the best male tennis players in the world before his retirement in 1951. Billie Jean King was also a strong advocate of women's rights and gender equality in tennis. Hence, this match was more than just an exhibition match. After Court's defeat, the entire pressure was on Billie Jean King's shoulders to prove both Riggs and the male chauvinists wrong. King wasn't just representing the female tennis players here but the entire fraternity of women who deserved equality in what was deemed to be a man's world. She accepted the challenge to defend women's tennis, as well as the feminist movement.

The Match

'The Battle of the Sexes' was a grand affair that was televised in the US. There was a carnival-like atmosphere when the day of the match finally arrived after so much hype. On 20 September 1973, Bobby Riggs and Billie Jean King faced off at the Houston Astrodome as the entire tennis world watched with bated breath.

King's Strategy

Modern tennis matches are not won by skill or talent alone. Unless a robust strategy is in place, it is tough to beat strong opponents in any sport. Riggs looked clueless as King made him run around with her exquisite lobs and drop shots. This strategy paid off, as Riggs became tired. King dominated the match and crushed both Riggs and his ego in a straight sets victory 6–4, 6–3, 6–3 as a huge global audience watched and cheered.

The Battle of the Sexes: A Bold Shift

The Iconic Victory

This was a huge moment in tennis, and a cultural milestone had been reached that would work wonders for women's sports in the future. The resistance to women's participation in many sports was smashed by Billie Jean King's win, and this led to the recognition of gender equality and women's empowerment in sports. Billie Jean King famously said after the match that it wasn't about winning at tennis but about showing that women were confident, strong, and equal.

However, it isn't always easy to defeat a fellow male tennis player because of the considerable advantages a man possesses in terms of physical strength and power. Ask the Williams sisters, and they'll tell you.

The Challenge by the Williams Sisters

Probably inspired by Billie Jean King's famous victory at the 'Battle of the Sexes' and eager to write their names into tennis history books as well, in 1998, Serena and Venus

Williams claimed that they could beat any male player who was ranked 200 or below.

Challenge Accepted

A German tennis player named Karsten Braasch, who was ranked 203 on the ATP Tour, accepted the challenge. A friendly match was mutually agreed upon, where Braasch would play each of the sisters in a match comprising a single set. The Williams sisters were relatively confident of defeating Braasch, who was also notorious for smoking cigarettes and having a beer or two before matches. Now, that's a strange fitness regimen for sure.

The Match

In an anticlimax of sorts, Karsten Braasch defeated both the Williams sisters on court, beating Venus 6–2 and Serena 6–1 in the respective matches. Not to be deterred, the Williams sisters then revised their claim, stating they could beat any male player ranked below 350. Never give up is a key lesson in tennis, after all.

Key Lessons

While the matches between Braasch versus the Williams sisters would have been retained in public memory had the outcome been slightly different, like in the case of Billie Jean King versus Bobby Riggs, there are key lessons to be learnt from both these episodes in tennis.

- Tennis is a great leveller.
- When you are playing for a cause rather than personal glory or pride, even the impossible can be achieved.

- Never underestimate someone.
- Always have a strategy in place before a tennis match.

THE PHYSICAL ASPECT OF PROFESSIONAL TENNIS

There is no doubt that modern tennis is physically demanding. The physical aspect of tennis is something that cannot be ignored at the topmost level. Without a high level of physical fitness, a professional player has no chance of survival on the tennis court today. To survive in tennis, you need these five attributes:

- Strength and power
- Speed
- Endurance
- Agility
- Coordination

All the shots in tennis, including those big serves and aces, volleys, lobs, smashes, and rallies, require a combination of these five elements.

10

INDIAN TENNIS

The immense popularity of tennis today is undeniable. Lawn tennis is one of the most popular sports globally, with a total viewership of approximately one billion people. What is interesting is that about 41 million fans are from India, even though there are no Indians in the top 100 Singles rankings currently. However, the future looks promising on that front as well.

As of March 2025, Sumit Nagal is India's highest-ranked Singles player, having earned a spot in the Top 150 rankings. There are 6 male Indian players who have broken into the Top 100 rankings: Rohan Bopanna (22), Yuki Bhambri (44), N. Sriram Balaji (64), Rithvik Bollipalli (74), Arjun Kadhe (86), and Jeevan Nedunchezhiyan (94).

Indian tennis players like Leander Paes, Mahesh Bhupathi, and Sania Mirza have won several Grand Slam titles in Doubles and Mixed Doubles. However, a Singles title has remained elusive. To date, no Indian player has ever won a Grand Slam Singles title in tennis in either the men's or women's category. The guys who have come within sniffing distance were Ramanathan Krishnan, his son Ramesh Krishnan, and Vijay Amritraj, all of whom managed to reach the quarter-finals of Grand Slam tournaments in Singles before bowing out.

The first popular Doubles team from India was undoubtedly the dynamic and dashing brothers from south India – Vijay Amritraj and Anand Amritraj. Although the duo never won a Grand Slam title, they reached the semi-finals of Wimbledon in 1976 in the men's Doubles.

Leander Peas created history when he won an Olympic bronze medal in the men's Singles at the 1996 Atlanta

Leander Paes

Mahesh Bhupathi

Olympic Games. He became the first Asian in Olympic history to win a medal in tennis and the only Indian tennis player to achieve this feat to date. Leander Paes also entered the record books by becoming the only tennis player to compete in seven Olympic Games from 1992 to 2016.

The duo of Leander Paes and Mahesh Bhupathi and their phenomenal success in men's Doubles was instrumental in making tennis popular among Indian youth during their playing days, just like Sania Mirza inspired many young Indian girls to take up the sport.

In women's tennis, Sania Mirza is the only Indian tennis player to have achieved major success. Sania was the first Indian woman to break into the Top 100 of the WTA Singles ranking, to win a WTA Singles tournament, to win a WTA Finals in Doubles, and to win as many as 6 Grand Slam titles in Doubles and Mixed Doubles. Sania was also ranked No. 1 in women's Doubles, which was a tremendous achievement.

Sania Mirza

INDIAN TENNIS: A BRIEF HISTORY

The British first introduced tennis in India in the 1880s, during colonial rule. Tennis grew in India and then slowly spread across Asia. In 1885, the first tennis tournament was held in Lahore (now in Pakistan) in undivided India. Two more tennis tournaments were soon added. In 1887, the Bengal Lawn Tennis Championships began in Calcutta (now Kolkata), and in 1910, the All India Lawn Tennis

Championships started in Allahabad (now Prayagraj). British players won all these tournaments regularly and had tennis stars like T.D. Berrington and L.C. Ogbourne.

In 1915, the scenario changed in favour of local players when India had its first tennis champion in Mohd. Saleem of Lahore, undivided India, who won the Punjab Championships. From 1917 to 1926, Mohd. Saleem dominated this tennis tournament. Meanwhile, the Bengal Championships also had its first Indian winner in N.S. Iyer in 1917. 1919 witnessed the first time an Indian won the All India Lawn Tennis Championships when Mr Nagu lifted the title.

But Indian tennis players had entered Wimbledon prior to these events. B.K. Nehru was the first Indian tennis player to enter Wimbledon. Sadly, he gifted a walkover to his opponent in the second round. Sardar Nihal Singh was the second Indian who managed to enter the main draw of Wimbledon in 1908 and the first to actually play at Wimbledon. But he lost in the first round itself.

In 1920, a British member of the Indian Civil Service, Samuel Perry O'Donnell, became the first president of the All India Lawn Tennis Association, which was formed in Lahore. It was decided to hold an all India National Championships and to send an Indian team to participate in the prestigious Davis Cup. The first Indian tennis team for the Davis Cup was thus formed, with Mohd. Saleem, S.M. Jacob, L.S. Deane, and A.A. Fayzee.

The Indian Davis Cup team had a spectacular Davis Cup debut as it defeated a strong French team to progress to the semi-finals. After that, the Indian contingent was a regular feature at the Davis Cup with the emergence of good tennis players, such as A.H. Fayzee, who was the brother of A.A. Fayzee, Cotah Ramaswamy, and Krishna Prasad. India defeated top tennis-playing nations like France, Spain, Greece, Bulgaria, Romania, and Holland several times. Many members of the Indian Davis Cup team made it to the main draw of Wimbledon after this, but they could not progress beyond the Round of 16.

Thanks to India's brilliant performance at the 1924 Paris Olympics, international tennis stars like Bill Tilden and Henry Cochet came to India to participate in tennis tournaments.

1939 was a breakthrough year for Indian tennis as India's No. 1 player, Ghouse Mohd., reached the Wimbledon quarter-finals and lost to eventual champion Bobby Riggs, the same guy who lost the 'Battle of the Sexes' match to Billie Jean King.

No Indian tennis player has won a Grand Slam Singles final to date, although Ramanathan Krishnan won the Wimbledon junior title in 1954, his son Ramesh Krishnan won both the Wimbledon and the French Open junior titles in the late seventies, and Leander Paes won the Wimbledon junior title in 1990. Paes was also briefly ranked the No. 1 junior player in the world.

After the end of World War II, the AILTA introduced two new tournaments in India. The first was the Grass Court National Championships, and the second was the All India Hard Court Championships. The first tournament was open to international tennis players.

In 1946, India's first Grass Court National Championships were held at the South Club in Calcutta. The winner of this tournament was Sumant Misra. Misra, Dilip Bose, and Ramanathan Krishnan were the only Indian players to win this tournament from 1946 to 1955. Ramanathan Krishnan was clearly the best Indian tennis player as he won a record 8 titles. The foreign players who continued to dominate this tournament till 1976 included greats like Roy Emerson and Ilie Năstase.

It was the turn of the father-son duo of Ramanathan Krishnan and Ramesh Krishnan to carry forward the legacy of Indian tennis after the Fayzee brothers had done their bit. The Krishnans created an impact in different time periods. Ramanathan Krishnan was the highest seeded Indian ever, at No. 4, when he played the Wimbledon Championships in 1962. Ramanathan Krishnan took the Indian Davis Cup team to new heights and was largely responsible for India reaching the Davis Cup finals in 1966, but they lost to a strong Australian team.

1974 saw the mercurial Amritraj brothers, Vijay and Anand, take India to yet another Davis Cup final, where India was to play South Africa. Ramanathan Krishnan was the non-playing captain of this team, which also included Jasjit Singh and Shashi Menon. South Africa had the home advantage, but the Amritraj brothers were in top form, and so, it was a battle of equals. Tragically, as mentioned earlier, the Indian government led by Indira Gandhi refused to send the Indian team to South Africa because of the apartheid policies of South Africa, which were unacceptable to India. So, as India boycotted the final, South Africa won the Davis Cup final without a match being played.

In 1987, thanks to the Herculean efforts of Ramesh Krishnan, India reached the Davis Cup finals for a third time. India beat Australia en route to the finals, which they lost for a third time. A powerful Swedish team with the likes of Stefan Edberg and Mats Wilander lifted the title.

THE MAGNIFICIENT SEVEN: FAMOUS INDIAN TENNIS PLAYERS

Here are the nicknames given to some famous Indian tennis players and how they are known in tennis circles globally:

Name of Player	Nickname
Ramanathan Krishnan	Madras Magician
Vijay Amritraj	The Black Tornado
Ramesh Krishnan	Eastern Magic
Leander Paes and Mahesh Bhupathi	Indian Express/Lee-Hesh
Rohan Bopanna	Bofors
Sania Mirza	Sam

Ramanathan Krishnan

Indian tennis owes a huge debt to the Madras Magician, Ramanathan Krishnan, who brought Indian tennis into the spotlight on the global stage in the 1960s. He became the first Asian tennis player to win the junior Wimbledon title in 1954, defeating Ashley Cooper in the final, who would go on to win four Grand Slams later. Unfortunately, Ramanathan Krishnan's senior career did not reach the heights of his junior career, as he did not win a Grand Slam title. But he was the first consistent Indian performer in the Grand Slams, reaching the semi-finals of Wimbledon twice, in 1960 and 1961, as well as the French Open quarter-finals in 1962. In men's Doubles, he reached the quarter-finals of Wimbledon four times. Ramanathan Krishnan's most famous wins in tennis include the ones against the legendary Rod Laver in the 1959 Davis Cup tie against Australia and the 1961 Wimbledon quarter-final when he upset 12-time Grand Slam champion Roy Emerson. The most memorable Doubles match was the 1966 Davis Cup final against Australia. Although India lost the final, Ramanathan Krishnan partnered with Jaidip Mukerjea to beat the fancied pair of John Newcombe and Tony Roche, the reigning Wimbledon men's Doubles champions.

Vijay Amritraj

Vijay Amritraj is one of the greats on this list. After Ramanathan Krishnan retired, the baton passed on to Vijay Amritraj, who was mentored by Krishnan as a non-playing captain in the Davis Cup.

Vijay Amritraj is the only Indian tennis player who was ranked among the Top 20 in the world in men's Singles. Although he has never won a Grand Slam title, he has a total of 29 career titles. He was also a formidable force in men's Doubles, as he partnered with his brother, Anand Amritraj, to win 13 ATP titles. In 1976, the duo reached the Wimbledon semi-finals, where they lost to eventual champions Brian Gottfried and Raul Ramirez. Twice, the Amritraj brothers played a crucial role in India reaching the finals of the Davis Cup – in 1974 and 1987.

In men's Singles, Vijay Amritraj reached the quarter-finals of both Wimbledon and the US Open twice each time. He has defeated the best players in the world at the time, including Rod Laver, Björn Borg, Jimmy Connors, and John McEnroe. Nicknamed the Black Tornado, his biggest victories on the tennis court were when he beat John McEnroe at the 1984 Cincinnati Masters and defeated Björn Borg at the US Open. Vijay Amritraj has been inducted into the International Tennis Hall of Fame in the contributor category.

Ramesh Krishnan

Like father, like son! This phrase sums it up perfectly when one describes Ramesh Krishnan's tennis journey. Ramesh Krishnan won the Wimbledon junior title in 1979, just as his father had done, but went one step ahead by winning the French Open junior title as well. That's called expansion of the family business. Ramesh Krishnan also had a good outing at the senior level by winning 8 ATP Singles titles in his playing career. In 1986, he won the ATP Challenger title in Schenectady, USA, by beating a young Andre Agassi in the final. Ramesh Krishnan also reached the quarter-finals of three Grand Slams: Wimbledon in 1986, and the 1981 and 1987 US Opens. He was also part of the Indian team that reached the Davis Cup final in 1987. In 1992, just a year before he retired, Ramesh Krishnan partnered with a young kid who went by the name of Leander Paes to reach the men's Doubles quarter-finals at the 1992 Barcelona Olympics. The torch or baton of Indian tennis was thus handed over to the future star. Ramesh Krishnan was honoured with the Padma Shri by the Indian Government for his contribution to Indian tennis.

Leander Paes

Arguably India's most famous tennis player, Leander Paes conquered the US Open and Wimbledon junior titles before he turned professional in 1991. It took him just five more years to become the first superstar of Indian tennis by winning an Olympic bronze medal in the men's Singles at the Atlanta 1996 Olympics. Leander Paes became a household name in India after this.

There was cause to celebrate, as this was India's first individual medal at the Olympics since wrestler K.D. Jadhav won a bronze medal way back in 1952. Although his life-changing moment came thanks to his performance in Singles, Leander Paes carved a name for himself in Doubles. Paes did win 1 ATP Singles title in his career before he focused entirely on Doubles. In 1998, he won the New Haven ATP tournament by defeating World No. 1, American Pete Sampras, in straight sets 6–3, 6–4.

Leander Paes is regarded as one of the most successful tennis players in Doubles in tennis history, having won a total of 8 men's Doubles Grand Slam titles. In fact, he achieved his Career Grand Slam in men's Doubles, as well as Mixed Doubles, having won all four Grand Slams in each category, which is a stupendous achievement. He is one of only three men in the Open Era to achieve a Career Grand Slam in both men's Doubles and Mixed Doubles. Let's take a detailed look at his men's Doubles Grand Slam titles:

Year	Men's Doubles Partner	Grand Slam Title
1999	Mahesh Bhupathi	Wimbledon, French Open
2001	Mahesh Bhupathi	French Open
2006	Martin Damm	US Open
2009	Lukáš Dlouhý	French Open, US Open
2012	Radek Št pánek	Australian Open
2013	Radek Št pánek	US Open

Leander Paes also has an impressive record in Mixed Doubles at Grand Slams, having won 10 titles.

Year	Mixed Doubles Partner	Grand Slam Title
1999	Lisa Raymond	Wimbledon
2003	Martina Navratilova	Australian Open, Wimbledon
2008	Cara Black	US Open
2010	Cara Black	Australian Open, Wimbledon
2015	Martina Hingis	Australian Open, US Open, Wimbledon
2016	Martina Hingis	French Open

In 1999, Leander Paes was ranked the No. 1 Doubles tennis player in the world. He also has the record of most Doubles wins at the Davis Cup. The recipient of the

Padma Shri and the Padma Bhushan, India's highest civilian honours, Leander Paes was inducted into the International Tennis Hall of Fame in 2024.

'The Indian Express' Leander–Mahesh Win Wimbledon

Mahesh Bhupathi

The Indian Express duo of Mahesh Bhupathi and Leander Paes won 3 prestigious Grand Slams in men's Doubles together to take Indian tennis to new heights. But Mahesh Bhupathi has the unique distinction of being the first Indian tennis player to win a Grand Slam title. He wrote his name in the record books in 1997 after winning the French Open Mixed Doubles by partnering with Japanese tennis player Rika Hiraki. After Leander Paes and Mahesh Bhupathi parted ways in men's Doubles, Mahesh Bhupathi partnered with Max Mirnyi in 2002 to win the US Open men's Doubles title. His career boasts 4 Grand Slams men's Doubles titles and 8 Mixed Doubles triumphs at Grand Slams, establishing himself as a tennis legend in his own right.

Year	Men's Doubles Partner	Grand Slam Title
1999	Leander Paes	Wimbledon, French Open
2001	Leander Paes	French Open
2002	Max Mirnyi	US Open

Year	Mixed Doubles Partner	Grand Slam Title
1997	Rika Hiraki	French Open
1999	Ai Sugiyama	US Open
2000	Virginia Ruano Pascual	French Open
2002	Elena Likhovtseva	French Open
2003	Lindsay Davenport	Wimbledon
2006	Martina Hingis	Australian Open
2009	Sania Mirza	Australian Open
2012	Sania Mirza	French Open

Rohan Bopanna

Rohan Bopanna is the only Indian male tennis player to win a Grand Slam title other than Leander Paes and Mahesh Bhupathi. He won the 2017 French Open Mixed Doubles title in partnership with Canadian female tennis player Gabriela Dabrowski. In 2024, a 43-year-old Rohan Bopanna repeated his Grand Slam success to win the men's Doubles title at the Australian Open by teaming up with Australian Matthew Ebden. He became the oldest male tennis player to ever win a Grand Slam title and the oldest tennis player to reach the World No. 1 ranking in Doubles. A year earlier, Bopanna also became the oldest tennis player to win an ATP Masters 1000 title. He teamed up with Ebden to win the 2023 Indian Wells Open title when he was 43 years old.

Sania Mirza

The biggest achievement in Indian women's tennis used to be Nirupama Sanjeev becoming the first woman to win a Grand Slam match at the 1998 Australian Open. After that, there was nothing to write home about till a certain Sania Mirza arrived on the tennis circuit.

Sania Mirza began her tennis journey by winning the Wimbledon girls' Doubles title in 2003. She partnered with Alisa Kleybanova to beat the favourites, Maria Sharapova and Tamarine Tanasugarn, in the final. Two years later, Sania became the first Indian woman Singles player to win a WTA title, playing on home turf to win the Hyderabad Open in 2005. To date, she is the only Indian woman to win a WTA Singles event. This was followed by 43 WTA Doubles titles. Four years after her first WTA triumph, Sania Mirza won her first Grand Slam title, becoming the only Indian woman to achieve this feat when she won the 2009 Mixed Doubles title by partnering with Mahesh Bhupathi. In 2011, the duo won the French Open Mixed Doubles title as well. In 2014, Sania clinched her third Mixed Doubles Grand Slam by partnering with Brazilian tennis player Bruno Soares to win the US Open.

The Rise Of Santina

2015 witnessed a legendary partnership in women's tennis as Sania Mirza and Swiss legend Martina Hingis teamed up to play Doubles. Fans called the duo Santina. They went on to complete an amazing 44-match winning streak together, proving to be a potent force in women's Doubles. The duo won three back-to-back Grand Slam women's Doubles titles in Wimbledon and the US Open in 2015 and the French Open in 2016. Sania Mirza also reached the No. 1 in WTA Doubles rankings during this period, a historic feat and the first Indian woman to achieve this. She has also represented India in international tennis competitions, winning medals at the Commonwealth Games, Asian Games, and Afro-Asian Games. She fell just short of a bronze medal at the 2016 Rio Olympics, losing in the semi-finals. Apart from putting Indian women's tennis on the world map, Sania has also inspired countless girls in India to take up tennis as a sport. She has been a huge inspiration and mentor for the current crop of women tennis players from India, like Maaya Rajeshwaran, Karman Kaur Thandi, and Ankita Raina, among others.

Apart from these magnificent seven, other players who deserve a special mention for taking Indian tennis forward are Ghaus Mohammad, Jasjit Singh, Premjit Lall, Jaidip Mukerjea, Zeeshan Ali, and Somdev Devvarman.

OTHER WOMEN TENNIS PLAYERS IN INDIA

- Rushmi Chakravarthi: Rushmi's most impressive performance was in the Afro-Asian Games in 2003, where she won four medals, including two golds, and at the 2010 Commonwealth Games, when she won the bronze medal in women's Doubles with Sania Mirza. Rushmi made her professional tennis debut in 2005 in the WTA Tour Sunfeast Open in Kolkata. She holds the record for the most ITF Women's Circuit championships won by an Indian woman, with 45 titles.

- Ankita Raina: In 2018, Ankita became the sixth Indian woman to break into the WTA top-200 rankings in Singles. Her best ranking was 160 in 2020. She broke into the top-100 in Doubles after she won the Phillip Island Trophy in Melbourne in 2021, making her the second Indian woman, after Sania Mirza, to win a WTA Tour trophy.
- Karman Kaur Thandi: Tipped to be a potential Top 50 player in women's tennis in the near future, Karman Kaur Thandi has risen consistently in the WTA rankings in recent times.

Maaya Rajeshwaran: The Indian Prodigy Mentored By Rafael Nadal

Maaya Rajeshwaran is a 16-year-old tennis sensation from India who is dubbed to be the next Indian star. Having trained at the Rafael Nadal Tennis Academy in Mallorca, Maaya has had the best training possible after a year-long full scholarship at the academy. She was selected by the academy after her exceptional performance at the WTA 125 Mumbai Open. A picture of Maaya training under the watchful eyes of the legendary Rafa went viral on social media, causing great excitement among Indian tennis fans.

Here's all that you need to know about the next big thing in Indian tennis.

- Maaya was born in Coimbatore, Tamil Nadu, on 12 June 2009. Her tennis journey began accidentally, as she picked up a tennis racket out of curiosity at an after-school activity. Her natural talent for the sport was soon revealed, and at age ten, Maaya decided to pursue a professional tennis career, thanks to backing from a supportive family. Her first coach was former India No. 1, K.G. Ramesh. Then, she trained under coach Manoj Kumar at the Pro Serve Tennis Academy.
- Maaya's breakthrough moment came at the L&T Mumbai Open in 2025, a WTA 125 tournament held annually in February. She entered the tournament as a wild card and stunned everyone to reach the semi-finals, beating players like Iryna Shyamanovich of Belarus, who was ranked No. 225, and Zarina Diyas of Kazakhstan, a former top 50 player in the WTA. Thanks to this exceptional performance, Maaya's WTA ranking shot up to 646, making her the youngest Indian to reach this milestone in tennis.
- Maaya's idol is Belarusian female tennis player Aryna Sabalenka, and her aggressive play is inspired by Sabalenka's style. Maaya spends a lot of time studying Sabalenka's moves. Sania Mirza is also a big inspiration for Maaya, and she has expressed her desire to replicate Sania's success.

Thankfully, the popularity of tennis in India has seen a dramatic surge over the past few decades. Players like Sumit

India's First Woman Tennis Player

Rita Davar was the first Indian female tennis player. Born on 3 June 1935, she was the first Indian to reach a tennis Grand Slam final. Davar met Fenny ten Bosch in the final of 1952 Wimbledon Girls' Singles and also had a few match points to create history. But she squandered those opportunities to lose the final 5–7, 6–1, 7–5.

In 1955, Davar partnered with Ramanathan Krishnan in the Mixed Doubles event to reach the third round at Wimbledon. In 1956, after losing in the first round of the qualifying draw, she married a German national and faded away to oblivion.

Nagal, Ramkumar Ramanathan, Prajnesh Gunneswaran, Ankita Raina, and many other Indian tennis players continue to perform well. As fans of Indian tennis, we can be quietly hopeful of winning the Davis Cup and having our own champion of a Grand Slam Singles title soon. Hanging on in quiet desperation is also the Indian way.

11

FUN FACTS, RECORDS, AND TENNIS STATS

WHEELCHAIR TENNIS

Brad Parks created wheelchair tennis in California in 1976. Parks was a former acrobatic skier who was paralysed in a skiing accident that took place in the same year. During his recovery process, Parks experimented by striking tennis balls with a racket while confined to his wheelchair. That's when he was struck by a fantastic idea that led to the birth of wheelchair tennis. Parks collaborated with physical therapist Jeff Minnebraker to create this unique sport and promoted it in the United States. Today, it is a popular wheelchair sport that has found a place in the Olympics, too.

Since 1985, the World Team Cup for wheelchair tennis has been held annually. The United States has dominated this competition by winning it a record nine times, from 1985 through 1991, and in 1995 and 1997. Countries other than the USA that have won the Wheelchair Tennis World Team Cup include the Netherlands, Belgium, Great Britain, Russia, Spain, France, Sweden, Australia, China, Japan, and Israel, among others, depending on the three divisions. For example, in 2025, Japan won the men's title while the Netherlands won the women's and quad titles.

Since 2007, wheelchair tennis became an integral part of the Grand Slams as well and has been played at all four Majors. There are three categories, namely Men, Women, and Quads, with Singles and Doubles events featuring in each category. The Quads category is the latest in wheelchair tennis and is also known as Mixed at the Olympics. It has been devised for players with a considerable loss of function in at least one upper limb. But this division can also feature several infirmities, except quadriplegia, a condition that makes it impossible to play tennis.

> Quadriplegia is also called tetraplegia and refers to paralysis that affects all four limbs, the torso, and the pelvic organs. This is usually caused by a high cervical spinal cord injury, but brain damage can also be a probable cause. Quadriplegia affects breathing and bladder/bowel control.

Quad players are sometimes seen taping their tennis rackets to their hands because of the loss of function, and some players are allowed to use motorized wheelchairs as well. Wheelchair tennis is a great symbol of the inclusivity of tennis. The rules are the same as regular tennis, but the only exception to the rules is that the ball is allowed to bounce twice, instead of just once. Thanks to wheelchair tennis, athletes with disabilities have a chance to display their talent and compete at the highest level of the sport.

THE BLACK PANTHER

American tennis player Arthur Ashe is the first black player to become a part of the US Davis Cup team. He became the first black player not only to win the US Open Men's Singles title, but also Wimbledon and the US Open.

Arthur Ashe

RICOCHETING RACKET FACTS

- The weights of tennis rackets range from seven ounces, or 200 grams, when unstrung to about 12.6 ounces, or 360 grams, when strung. However, this weight may vary according to player preferences in the recreational, amateur, or professional modes. While recreational players normally prefer rackets with an average weight of 250 to 350 grams unstrung, 270 to 295 grams is the preferred choice of advanced players. But even this has a catch to it, as some players, like beginners with less strength, may prefer lighter tennis rackets that are below 280 grams unstrung to give them better manoeuvrability on court. Heavier rackets, over 300 grams unstrung, give professional players more power and stability.
- **The Most Expensive Tennis Racket:** An ordinary Slazenger lawn tennis racket is the world's most expensive racket. Wait! This racket belonged to tennis legend Fred Perry, who played Wimbledon with it. In June 1997, Perry's racket sold at an auction at Christie's in London for an astonishing $37,724. That's no ordinary racket!
- **Smashing Rackets:** We have often seen tennis players throw or smash their rackets in the midst of the game as an act of frustration, displeasure, rage, or all of the above. But tennis players have learnt in time to keep their anger in check for fear of being disqualified from the tournament.
- In 1995, British player Tim Henman earned the distinction of being the first player in tennis history

to be disqualified from Wimbledon. Henman's offence was hitting a ball in frustration that accidentally hit a ball girl. Henman apologized to the ball girl later and also gifted her a bouquet of flowers.

- In 2000, Serbian player Goran Ivanišević became the first player in tennis history to lose at Wimbledon because he accidentally smashed all three of his rackets.
- In 2020, another Serbian named Novak Djokovic found himself being disqualified from the US Open after he hit a ball in frustration that went and struck a line woman's neck by accident. Djokovic apologized after the incident and also later in an online post.
- **Most Successful Tennis Rackets:** Head tennis rackets were miles ahead of the others in 2021, with the most ATP tournaments won playing with them. Players using Head rackets won 29 ATP titles. The second was Wilson tennis rackets, with 13 wins, Yonex with 8, Babolat with 7, and Tecnifibre with 4. However, Wilson was the ladies' choice in 2021 as these rackets helped women players win the most WTA matches, with 22 wins. After Wilson, Babolat had the most wins in the WTA with 17, Yonex with 16, Head with 12, and Tecnifibre with 5.
- In 2025, top players like Jannik Sinner used a Head Speed MP, Novak Djokovic used a Head Speed Pro, and Carlos Alcaraz used the Babolat Pure Aero 98 tennis racket. Other popular rackets preferred by the professionals include the Wilson Blade, Head Gravity, and Yonex Percept.

SHORTEST TENNIS MATCHES

- At the 1946 Surrey Hard Court Championships, Jack Harper defeated J. Sandiford 6–0, 6–0 in a best-of-three-sets match. The match went into the record books as the shortest men's Singles match played in tennis history and lasted for only 18 minutes.
- The shortest recorded match for women's Singles was recorded in 1963 during the Eastern Grass Court Championships. Margaret Court blew away Darlene Hard in only 24 minutes to wrap up the match 6–1, 6–1.
- The shortest Grand Slam final took place at the 1988 French Open women's Singles final. Steffi Graf brushed aside the challenge from Natasha Zvereva in just 34 minutes, winning the match 6–0, 6–0. Not exactly value for money for the spectators gathered for a French Open final. Un truc de ouf?

THE MOST ACES IN TENNIS

Swiss legend Roger Federer has smashed 11,478 aces en route to becoming a legend of the game. But Mr Federer is only in the third spot on the list of tennis players with the most aces. American John Isner is perched on top of this special list with 14,260 aces.

THE MOST X FOLLOWERS

Novak Djokovic might be the one with the most Grand Slam Singles titles, but he's not in the Top 3 when it comes to the most followers on X, formerly known as Twitter.

Rafael Nadal has the most followers on X, with more than 39 million followers as of mid-2025. In second place is Serena Williams, with 27.6 million followers, followed by Roger Federer, with 24.9 million followers.

THE FASTEST SERVE IN WOMEN'S TENNIS

Sabine Lisicki of Germany's serve of 210km/h is the fastest ever recorded in women's tennis.

THE LARGEST CROWD AT A TENNIS MATCH

The largest recorded crowd in a tennis match was observed at the Cape Town Stadium in South Africa, where Roger Federer played Rafael Nadal. 51,954 spectators were present for this charity match, and more than $3.5 million was raised for children's education in Africa. That's a good crowd for a good cause!

THE FLOATING COURT

Roger Federer and Rafael Nadal once played an exhibition match in Doha Bay, Qatar, on a specially made floating court. That must have been fun!

HOLY COW

Swiss cows are known to be among the finest in the world. Hence, Roger Federer was given the strange prize of a milking cow named Juliet when he won the Swiss Open in 2003. But Roger was obviously no Romeo as he didn't have a clue what to do with Juliet. In 2013, Federer received the same gift again. This time, he received a cow named

Desiree. Federer decided to give both the cows to a dairy farmer as milking cows and milking points on the tennis court require totally different skills.

THE BATTLE OF THE SURFACES

Tennis has come a long way from its early days when it was played on hard surfaces such as wood or stone. Today, a tennis court is created by using different types of surfaces, like grass, clay, hard, and carpet. Each surface considerably affects the playing style of tennis because the ball tends to move faster on some surfaces and slower on others. The 'Battle of the Surfaces' was an interesting three-setter exhibition match that was held in Spain on 2 May 2007 between Roger Federer and Rafael Nadal. The court on this special surface was unique as it was half-grass and half-clay, basically being split between grass on one side and clay on the other. This was a sort of symbolic rivalry between the two greats, as Nadal was a master on clay, while Federer excelled on grass. Rafael Nadal proved his mastery on clay, and that even half a surface was enough for him as he defeated Roger Federer 7–5, 4–6, 7–6 (12–10) in a keenly contested match.

THE OLDEST TENNIS COURT

Tennis is still played at the oldest tennis court in the world. Between 1526 and 1529, Cardinal Wolsey built the first modern tennis court for his personal use at Hampton Court Palace, England. King Henry VIII was a fantastic tennis player in his younger days and spent long hours on this tennis court. In fact, the two most powerful kings who reigned in the 16th century, Henry VIII of Britain and Francis I of France, were exceptional tennis players.

THE HIGHEST TENNIS COURT

The world's highest tennis court can be found at the Burj Al Arab, a luxurious hotel that's located in Dubai. This special tennis court is 211 metres above the ground.

RECORD OF THE DON

Don Budge is the only male tennis player who has won 6 Grand Slam titles back to back. The Don began with the 1937 Wimbledon title and continued his winning spree until the 1938 US Open.

SLAM QUEEN

The most successful female player in Grand Slam tennis history is Serena Williams. Serena has won 23 Grand Slam Singles titles, 14 women's Doubles titles, and 2 Mixed Doubles titles. That's an astonishing 39 Grand Slam titles in total. However, when it comes to the maximum women's Singles Grand Slam titles, Margaret Court has won 24 Grand Slam Singles titles, just one more than Serena.

HIGHEST CAREER EARNINGS IN TENNIS

Novak Djokovic has the highest career earnings in tennis by winning an estimated $170 million in prize money, a figure that is still growing as Novak is still active in professional tennis. That's $35 million more than Rafael Nadal earned in his entire career, and who's in second place. Roger Federer is in third place, with career earnings of $131 million. No wonder they are called the 'Big Three'.

NOVAK'S ELECTRO MUSIC

When Serbian legend Novak Djokovic was a little boy and dreaming of becoming the greatest tennis player in the world, his coach at the time, a gentleman named Bogdan Obradovi introduced him to the music of the Beatles and a local Serbian rock band named Elektri ni Orgazam or Electro Orgasm. Obradovi got an electric guitar during tennis practice and played the famous song 'Everyone in Yugoslavia is playing rock n roll' by Electro Orgasm. Novak was having some trouble returning serves on the tennis court, and his musical coach wanted to show him that playing and listening to music could help the cause as they were similar to a return of serve. He instructed a young Novak that it was all about the rhythm and asked him to listen to the rhythm of the song and follow it. Only then would Novak find the rhythm in his movements on the tennis court, his return of serve, and his overall play. Obradovi taught Novak that music therapy really helped a tennis player and also introduced him to Beatles songs like 'Yesterday'. In fact, that Beatles number must have been on Novak's playlist, surely, when he was deported from Australia.

THE DJOKOVIC CHOCOLATE ALARM

Just like all other sportspersons, tennis players have to be very careful about their diet as tennis is a strenuous game that demands great fitness and an enormous amount of self-restraint when it comes to choice of food. Novak Djokovic once set a chocolate alarm on his phone to the precise minute so that he would know when a year had gone by since he last ate a piece of chocolate. Tennis is clearly not a sport for chocoholics.

NOVAK'S UNIQUE RECORD

Apart from his heroics at the Australian Open, Novak Djokovic is the only man in the history of tennis who has won all nine ATP Masters tournaments in his career. This displays his tennis talent and adaptability on all possible surfaces.

THE TENNIS BRACELET

Chris Evert lost her diamond bracelet on the court while she was playing at the 1987 US Open. This led to the term 'tennis bracelet' being coined as another name for a diamond bracelet. The loss of her bracelet must have affected six-time champion Chris Evert. She lost in the quarter-finals in a shock defeat to Lori McNeil, and this was the first time Evert had lost in the US Open before the semi-finals. This loss ended Chris Evert's streak of 17 consecutive semi-finals at the US Open. They don't call diamonds a woman's best friend for nothing!

THE POLO SHIRT DESIGN

Cotton polo shirts made their debut as tennis apparel. The modern polo shirt used in tennis was designed with the collar intentionally popped. This was to stop the harsh rays of the sun from burning the players' necks when they played tennis during the day. That is why it is advised that tennis courts must be aligned north-south to protect the tennis players on both ends from the direct rays of the sun.

TENNIS BALL FUN FACTS

- **Too Many Balls:** It takes just a little more than 58,000 tennis balls to cover one tennis court.
- **What's All the Fuzz?:** The fuzz on a tennis ball enhances wind resistance, which slows the ball down to help players volley for a longer period of time. Without the fuzz, most serves would be so fast that the tennis ball would simply fly off the court, giving the opponent no chance of returning the serve. As players strike the ball with the racket, the fuzz helps them control the ball by keeping it attached to the tennis racket for a wee bit longer, which is about a millisecond or two. That's why they say that every millisecond counts!
- **Perception of Colour:** A tennis ball poll on X from August 2023 revealed that people have varying views about the colour of tennis balls. 52% said it was green, 42% were of the opinion that it was yellow, and 6% said 'other'. This is all about human perception. Actually, the colour of the tennis ball is optic yellow, which is a fluorescent yellow, chosen for better visibility.
- **Tennis Ball Movement:** Did you know that the tennis ball is in action or in a state of movement for only about 20 minutes on average in a tennis match that lasts for two and a half hours?
- **Tennis Ball Sounds:** The sound of the tennis ball

being hit by a racket actually varies, as it is dependent on factors like the brand of the ball and the type of court surface.

- **Ball Velocity and Grunting:** A 2014 study conducted on NCAA Division I tennis players revealed that when a player grunts before making a groundstroke, it actually increases ball velocity by 3.8%, without an increase in the effort made in the shot or the cost of oxygen. This discovery suggests that grunting actually boosts performance at a tennis match and can be an effective performance-enhancing tennis strategy. Ball velocity was measured with a radar gun during this study, and physiological responses like heart rate and the consumption of oxygen were also factored in.

TENNIS AND ENDURANCE CAPACITY

Another study revealed that playing tennis results in a higher endurance capacity than activities like bike riding and jogging. Single longitudinal research was conducted, and 38 middle-aged volunteers were chosen for this study. They were divided into four groups, namely biking, tennis, running, and a control group. The group was made to exercise over a period of 20 weeks, thrice a week for half an hour. The end results displayed that while the control group remained unchanged, cycling brought about an increase in endurance capacity by 14.8% while running increased it by 13.3%. But the point to be noted here in terms of endurance capacity is that 30 minutes of tennis is only about 30% of the time a tennis player spends on court. To explain endurance levels better, keep in mind that a player runs an average of three miles during a tennis match. However, that is a tough three miles of continuous back and forth movement carrying a tennis racket because of the restricted length of a tennis court, say, as compared to a football field.

AN EFFICIENT CALORIE BURNER

According to data released by Healthstatus.com, an hour of tennis played by an individual helps a person weighing 160 pounds burn about 441 calories. What makes tennis a great calorie burner is that a tennis match involves running to play those shots and returns and long rallies that consume a lot of energy.

TENNIS BOOSTS CARDIOVASCULAR HEALTH

Tennis is considered a great option if you wish to improve your cardiovascular health. As tennis matches can stretch up to three hours or more, aerobic system health and muscle endurance are greatly impacted. People who have played tennis regularly have been exposed to limited instances of cardiovascular disease like hypertension and coronary artery complications. The heart rate of an adult ranges from about 60 to 100 beats per minute. A low heart rate means a person's heart is in good condition and cardiovascular health is good. To illustrate the point, Björn Borg had a resting heart rate of 35 beats per minute at the peak of his career. This was the result of years of tennis training leading to better cardiovascular health.

TENNIS ELBOW

An inflammation of the tendons joining the muscles of the forearm on the outside of the elbow is called tennis elbow. A tennis elbow is known to affect almost 50% of tennis players, caused by wrist and arm motions that are repetitive in a tennis match. The outside of the elbow is usually the main affected area, although the wrist and the forearm can also be affected. The symptom is often pain, and treatment involves rest, medication, and physical therapy.

TENNIS FOR TWO

Tennis for Two is considered the very first video game that arrived in 1958. A nuclear scientist named William Higinbotham developed this electronic tennis game, which was the ancestor of today's popular video games. The game was first demonstrated on 18 October 1958, and there was a large gathering at Brookhaven National Laboratory as visitors lined up to play Tennis for Two. It was played by two players who used separate controllers linked to an analogue computer with an oscilloscope serving as a screen.

TENNIS FACTS FROM THE USA

- Tennis is an immensely popular sport in the USA, which has naturally produced some of the best champions in tennis history over the years. In 2017, almost 18 million people played tennis in the United States in some capacity or the other. In 2025, this figure grew to a mammoth 25.7 million people, according to data published in February 2025 by the

United States Tennis Association (USTA). That's an 8% increase from 23.8 million tennis players in 2024. One in every 12 Americans plays tennis, which is reflective of the passion for tennis in the United States.

- Naturally, with so many tennis players in a single country, amateur, professional, or recreational, having abundant tennis courts is an absolute must. The United States doesn't disappoint there as well, as there are an estimated 2,70,000 tennis courts in the country as per the Tennis Industry Association (TIA). These courts are scattered across various locations – residential properties, community areas, apartment complexes, and tennis training facilities. Some of the locations might seem strange to the outsider, with tennis courts in an Iowa family farm, on the ledges of Alcatraz, or on the beaches of Lake George. Why, even the White House has a tennis court for the recreational purposes of its residents.
- 2020 saw a growth of 40% in tennis racket sales in the USA according to the TIA, which helps monitor the US tennis industry. The market for tennis rackets is poised for significant growth and is expected to grow at a compound annual growth rate (CAGR) of 6.8% from 2025 to 2030. The key factors driving this exponential growth are:

    - The presence of a strong tennis culture
    - The presence of professional tournaments and their extended coverage
    - Rising health awareness in the USA
    - Technological advancements made in tennis

- Interest among American youth
- Strong marketing and media

- Tennis players have to run at least twice more the distance than most American football players in each match.

THE YOUNGEST WORLD NO. 1 IN TENNIS

The record for being the youngest ever male tennis player to become the No. 1 tennis player in the world belongs to Australian Lleyton Hewitt. He did so when he was only 20 years and 268 years old. Martina Hingis holds the record for being the youngest No. 1 female tennis player in the world as she achieved this when she was only 16 years old.

The First Winners of Each Grand Slam Event

Champion	Grand Slam
Rodney Heath	Australian Open
H. Briggs	French Open
Spencer Gore	Wimbledon
Richard Sears	US Open

THE FIRST CALENDAR YEAR GRAND SLAM WINNER

American Don Budge was the first player in tennis history to win the Calendar Year Grand Slam in 1938. Don simply refused to budge and won all the Grand Slams that year.

THE RETURN OF THE ROCKET

Australian Rod Laver is the only male tennis player to achieve the historic Calendar Year Grand Slam twice in men's Singles. He did this in 1962, first as an amateur and then in the Open Era as a professional in 1969. This is one of the greatest achievements, not only in tennis, but also in sporting history. When Rod Laver decided to turn professional in 1963, he was banned from Grand Slams for five years, but he still returned to dominate the early Open Era, when professional tennis players were finally allowed to play in the Grand Slams. No wonder he was nicknamed 'Rocket'.

THE BIG TWO IN MEN'S TENNIS

The Big Three of tennis disbanded after the retirements of Federer and Nadal, although Djokovic is still going strong. However, the emergence of a new world order in men's tennis in Spaniard Carlos Alcaraz and Italian Jannik Sinner has reignited the rivalry. Alcaraz leads this rivalry 10–5 currently, but in 2025, Alcaraz was miles ahead, winning four of the five head-to-head matches. But the beauty of this rivalry is the absence of a third challenger. Djokovic consistently lost in the semi-finals of all the Grand Slams in 2025 to mostly either of these two young geniuses. In fact, Djokovic was denied his 25th Grand Slam title because Carlos Alcaraz began the 2026 tennis season by winning the Australian Open, defeating Novak Djokovic in the final to complete a Career Grand Slam at 22 years and 272 days old, making him the youngest man in history to achieve this feat.

Carlos Alcaraz v Novak Djokovic Condensed Match | Australian Open 2026 Final

Alcaraz has already set a world record by reaching the quarter-final of a Grand Slam 13 times in only 19 appearances. He became the youngest to achieve this feat before 23, breaking Boris Becker's world record. Meanwhile, 23-year-old Jannik Sinner became the first Italian man to win Wimbledon in the Open Era. Between them, these two, who are also World No. 1 and World No. 2, respectively, have also won the last eight Grand Slam titles, by winning four apiece. But the gulf between them and their nearest rivals is a wide one. Here's hoping we can have another Big Three in the near future.

ALMOST UNBREAKABLE TENNIS RECORDS OF THE OPEN ERA

While records are often set and broken in sport, there are a few records that set the bar and may be impossible to break, simply because of the scale and magnitude of the achievement. Here are the Top 10 records of tennis set in the Open Era that look unbreakable as of now.

10. 93 Grand Slam Main-Draw Appearances

At No. 10 is American Venus Williams's record of a stunning 93 Grand Slam appearances in the main draw. The senior Williams sister made her Grand Slam debut as a 16-year-old at the French Open in 1997. Venus played her last Grand Slam in the 2023 US Open as a 43-year-old, more than 26 years since her debut. This record looks tough to break because of the sheer longevity of Venus's career and because tennis careers are much shorter these days.

9. A Gap of More Than 17 Years Between Grand Slam Wins

The first Grand Slam title that Serena Williams won was the 1999 US Open, when she was just 17 years old. The last Grand Slam title that she won was the 2017 Australian Open as a 35-year-old, making her the oldest woman to win a Grand Slam title in the Open Era, and that, too, when she was eight weeks pregnant with her first child. The record that will be tough to break is the astonishing time span of 17 years and 4 months between her first and last Grand Slam win, which was also her 23rd Grand Slam title. Rafael Nadal is next on this list, with a 17-year-difference between his 2005 and 2022 French Open wins, his first and his last. The difference between him and Serena is just 4 months.

8. *Most Consecutive Grand Slam Semi-Finals*

Roger Federer's record of making it to 23 consecutive Grand Slam semi-finals is unmatched by anyone in tennis history, and it looks like no one will be able to surpass this record. Displaying remarkable consistency, Federer achieved this feat right from Wimbledon 2004 to the 2010 Australian Open. This streak was upset by Robin Soderling when he defeated Federer in the quarter-finals of the 2010 French Open.

7. *125-Match Winning Streak*

Chris Evert's amazing Open Era record of winning 125 matches in a row on clay stands to date. Chris Evert did not lose at Roland-Garros for almost six years between September 1973 and May 1979.

6. *Six Consecutive Years As No. 1*

American tennis player Pete Sampras is the only player who has ended six consecutive seasons as No. 1. Martina Navratilova and Jimmy Connors managed to do it five years in a row, and Steffi Graf, John McEnroe, and Roger Federer have become World No. 1 four times in a row. That's why this record looks so difficult to break. No one did it like Pistol Pete, who ended every year from 1993 to 1998 as the World No. 1 in men's tennis. He also won 10 Grand Slam titles during this period.

5. *Youngest Grand Slam Winner*

Martina Hingis holds the unique record of being the youngest winner of a Grand Slam at 16 years and 3 months.

It will take someone and something really special to beat that record for sure.

4. *Most Titles in Tennis*

No one comes close to Martina Navratilova when it comes to total or combined tennis titles won, and there's serious doubt if anyone will get close as well. Navratilova has won a mind-boggling 167 career Singles titles, which is a WTA record, narrowly beating Chris Evert's 157 career titles. But Navratilova has also won 187 Doubles titles and 10 Grand Slam Mixed Doubles trophies in her illustrious career, which takes the total tally to 354 titles. No tennis player in the history of the Open Era comes close, with even the guys far behind. John McEnroe is the best among the men, with a total career titles of 155, out of which 77 have come in Singles and 78 in Doubles.

Martina Navratilova absolutely loved smashing the tennis ball, as well as smashing records. Here are two of her other great records that seem invincible:

- She has the best win-loss record in a single tennis season, which is 86–1 or 98.85%. She achieved this in 1983.
- Navratilova has won 120 Singles matches at Wimbledon, and that's more than any other tennis player at any Grand Slam.

3. *Most Weeks Spent As No. 1*

Novak Djokovic was World No. 1 for as long as 428 weeks, beating Steffi Graf's record among both men and women. Graf had held the earlier record by being No. 1 in the world for 377 weeks.

2. *The Golden Grand Slam*

Steffi Graf's amazing record of being the only one to win the Golden Grand Slam is one of the greatest achievements in tennis. In 1988, Steffi Graf won all the Grand Slams, as well as the Olympic gold medal in Seoul. This feat is arguably the toughest record to beat in tennis.

1. *The Rafa Record At Roland-Garros*

The king of clay, Rafael Nadal, has several seemingly unbeatable records at the French Open, including 14 title victories. His winning percentage here is 97.4%, the highest of any tennis player at any Grand Slam.

12

BIZARRE FACTS OF TENNIS

WEIRD SUPERSTITIONS

Superstitions have existed from the early days of mankind, and tennis has had its fair share of superstitions as well. And some are dark and bizarre, too.

The psychology behind these tennis superstitions is normally threefold in nature.

- Many tennis players are known to be superstitious as a confidence booster before their matches.
- Superstitions give players a sense of stability and control when they play, as it affects their mental state in a positive manner.
- If a tennis player achieves success while observing a certain superstitious ritual, it can strengthen the belief that future success will also be brought about by observing the same.

However, having said that, it's still funny to think that tennis players are so superstitious when the game itself is in a state of continuous evolution. Here are some of the bizarre superstitions of tennis players.

- Five-time Wimbledon champion, Swedish legend Björn Borg, grew a lucky beard before he competed in his favourite Grand Slam and refused to shave till he was eliminated from the tournament. He continued this weird, sorry, beard tradition in all his back-to-back Wimbledon triumphs from 1976 to 1980. This was odd as Borg wasn't known for sporting facial hair normally. Beardo would have snapped him up as brand ambassador surely if he was playing today.
- During Wimbledon 2001, Serbian Goran Ivanišević used to watch Teletubbies every day, believing that they lifted his game. Goran also ate the same food at the same table at the same restaurant when he played at Wimbledon.
- One can have an entire chapter dedicated to the superstitions of the king of clay, Rafael Nadal. But we shall try and keep it short. Every time he won a tournament, Rafael Nadal would bite the trophy. Just a gentle bite, mind you. Rafa arranged his drink bottles in a precise alignment, like a fanatical worker at a soda bottle factory. He also wore the same socks and at the same height. Rafael Nadal is a superstitious Spaniard for sure. He always carried two bottles of water when he walked into the court, one of which was warm and the other cold. Rafa ensured that these bottles were always diagonally placed, facing the court, and had the labels pointed to his side of the net. Swiss star Roger Federer went one step further when it came to water bottles. He carried eight water bottles and eight tennis

rackets simply because eight was his lucky number. Rafa carried just one racket, but before he walked on to the court, he would always have his mandatory cold shower of 45 minutes, which energized him before a match. Rafa always spent time alone before a match to achieve the right frame of mind and engaged in meditation and breathing techniques. He tried not to step on the lines of his side of the tennis court. When he had to do so, he crossed the lines with his right foot always. After returning to his seat during games, Rafa always put his bag on the bench and placed his tournament ID face-up every time. Another quirk was that whenever he drank from his energy gel pouch, Rafa ripped off the top first and used just four gentle squeezes to move the gel to the mouth of the pouch. Add to that the constant face and hair wiping during a match, as well as the underwear-picking before he served. Rafa also had this strange habit of jumping each time the coin toss took place. Then, irrespective of whether he had won or lost the toss, he would race back to his line after that. During a changeover, Rafa waited till his opponent took his seat before he left the court. It's debatable if this was a polite gesture or superstition, however. Another of Rafa's famous rituals is using the same towel during matches. That towel must have been quite messy during those marathon five-setters at Roland-Garros, though. Use and throw, for sure!

- Serena Williams's sock and shoe routine was famous during her playing days. She would tie her shoelaces exactly the same way, use the same shower before her matches, and wear the same socks throughout the tournament. We aren't sure if those socks took a shower after the matches, though. Serena also insisted on bouncing the ball five times before her first serve. But maybe that ritual was to intimidate her opponent.

- When it comes to ball-bouncing superstitions and rituals, Novak Djokovic is the undisputed king. He surpassed his own record during Serbia's Davis Cup tie against Australia when he bounced the ball as many as 38 or 39 times before serving. We hope he didn't put his opponent to sleep!
- If Nadal ranks at the top when it comes to superstitions among the Big Three of tennis, Djokovic must be a close second. Novak insists that both his favourite poodles travel with him to Wimbledon as his lucky charms. This trend must have begun when Djokovic won Wimbledon with his poodles in tow.
- Djokovic was spotted wearing a strange device on his chest during the 2021 Italian Open, which had even the Italians zapped. Novak jokingly said it was a nanotechnology device that was his 'Iron Man' secret. Yeah, we believe you, Djoker!
- But wait, there's more! Novak's obsession with Bosnian Pyramid Water is legendary. He swears by the healing power of the water from the man-made pyramids, located in Bosnia and Herzegovina, and also consumes it on a regular basis. Here's hoping that it helps Djokovic win his elusive 25th Grand Slam Singles title that he's been chasing.
- While Djokovic is renowned in tennis for his 'Iron Man' power, even the shower isn't too far behind. While some players insist on using the same shower

as a lucky charm, the Serbian giant never uses the same shower twice at a tournament. More showers for more power!

- Gabriel Debru is a classic example of shower faithful. During the 2002 French Open, he religiously used the same shower after each match. This must have worked as he won the title.
- French tennis player Richard Gasquet was the nightmare of every ball boy and ball girl. Every time Gasquet won a point when he was serving, he demanded that he be given the same ball that had helped him win the point. His obsession with using the same winning ball for his next serve caused problems when the Frenchman lost a point while serving. It led to a time delay as Gasquet went through all the balls that were thrown at him till he thought he had found the ball that had helped him win his last serve.
- Slovakian female tennis player Dominika Cibulková had this strange habit of smelling tennis balls before she served. Smells like teen spirit or simply sniffing victory?
- The most bemusing one is saved for the last. Andre Agassi, revealed in his autobiography, *Open*, that he forgot to wear his underwear for the first match during the 1999 French Open, that he won. After that, Agassi decided to play the entire tournament 'commando style', without his underwear, and actually won the tournament in grand style.

THE KING OF GOOD TIMES

Once upon a time in tennis, a queen named Anne Boleyn was watching her husband, King Henry VIII, play a game of tennis. Rumour has it that she was suddenly arrested on suspicion of treason against the king. Henry's second wife, Anne, was imprisoned in the Tower of London and executed later. When she was being hanged, Henry was busy playing another tennis match.

WILD TENNIS

Have you heard of the Serengeti National Park in the Tanzanian Savannah? Many of you may have, but how many of you are aware of the unfenced tennis court that lies here? Playing tennis is certainly wild here, as your average spectators are antelopes, zebras, and lions, to name a few. Play at your own peril!

DEATH OF THE TENNIS KING

Scotland's King James I loved tennis so much that it brought about his demise. The early version of tennis that the Scottish king was addicted to featured balls and rackets, but they did not have ball boys or ball girls to fetch the balls in those days. As a result, good old James kept losing a lot of tennis balls during play, which disappeared into the sewage drain at the corner of the court at Blackfriars Monastery. Tennis began as a sport for monks, remember?

The loss of so many tennis balls is enough to make even a king angry, and James was no exception. He ordered that the offending sewage drain that was gulping down so many of his tennis balls be sealed with immediate effect. A king must always seek the decisions of his wise men, even if it means it's a harmless one like sealing a sewage drain, which is there for a purpose. This decision would haunt

James pretty badly as, a few days later, hired assassins broke into the palace to do what they do best – assassinate kings. As James ran away from these professional killers to continue his line, he entered the drainage system to give them the slip. He wanted to escape using the tennis court exit, forgetting totally that he had himself ordered it to be sealed. As his eyes greeted the newly sealed grate, James realized he was trapped. The killers eventually caught him, and that was the end of a passionate tennis player.

BRAZILIAN BALL DOGS

If only ball boys were there when King James was playing, he wouldn't have met with such a tragic death. Ball boys and girls are an integral part of tennis. But the Brazil Open tennis tournament in 2016 created tennis history when it replaced ball boys with stray dogs. These four former stray dogs, named Frida, Mel, Isabelle, and Costela, from the streets of Sao Paulo in Brazil, worked as ball dogs in an exhibition match played between Spanish tennis player Roberto Carballés Baena and Portuguese tennis player Gastão Elias. Wearing orange ribbons, these ball dogs were busy for almost half an hour, fetching wayward balls back to the tennis court. The dogs trained hard for several months for this new role, and this was a commendable effort to adopt abandoned street animals into sport.

THE CURIOUS CASE OF THE WIMBLEDON PINEAPPLE

The pineapple on top of the Wimbledon trophy represents no ordinary pineapple. In fact, it symbolizes the age-old tradition of English sailors placing pineapples on their gateposts after their return from long sea voyages. No one has a clue how tennis was linked to those long sea trips, but it's quite a cute tradition, so no one is complaining. Pineapples do go well with cream after all!

BOLAND'S GOLD

An Irish tennis player named John Pius Boland won 2 Olympic gold medals in tennis, completely by accident. Boland also became the first person to win the Olympic gold in tennis in a rather bizarre fashion. Boland was on holiday in Athens in 1896 and just chilling out when his friend persuaded him to sign up for the Olympics tennis Singles event. It certainly helped that this friend, named Thrasyvoalos Manaos, was the secretary of the Athens 1896 Organising Committee. Boland surprised everyone, including himself, when he played with leather-soled shoes with heels and still managed to win the competition. Boland decided to try his luck at the men's Doubles event at the Olympics as well. Since everybody else was taken, Boland teamed up with Friedrich Traun of Germany, a guy Boland had beaten in the first round of the Olympics' men's Singles. Surprise, surprise! Boland and Traun won the men's Doubles, too. That's what is called mixing business with pleasure to win two Olympic gold medals.

TONGUE STRATEGY

Boris Becker and Andre Agassi had a tennis rivalry that was fast and furious. After Becker had beaten Agassi in their first three contests and completed a hat-trick of wins, Andre was forced to think differently. Badly wanting to beat Boris Becker, Agassi studied tapes of their previous matches on repeat mode. Then, he finally observed something amazing. He discovered that Becker put out his tongue in a strange manner before he served. If the German's tongue was to the left of his mouth, he would serve wide. If Becker's tongue stayed in the centre of his mouth, the ball would be served in the centre. Armed with this new knowledge, Agassi went on to beat Becker, thanks to technology. After their playing days were over, Andre Agassi mentioned this strange fact to Boris Becker, who was so stunned that he almost fell off his chair.

TEN MOST BIZARRE MOMENTS IN TENNIS HISTORY

10. Italian Ice Cream

When in Rome, do as the Romans do! But not always, as British tennis player Tony Pickard discovered in 1963. That's when Pickard found out, much to his shock, that the organizers of the Italian Championships were not as serious as the ones at Wimbledon. Pickard was playing Kiwi player Ian Crookenden, and the match was so slow that both the spectators and the line judges were bored to death. In a crucial game point, Crookenden served, and the ball was at least 9 inches outside, as per Pickard. The umpire looked at the baseline judge for the call, but the good man had his back towards the tennis match and was buying an ice cream over the fence. Crookenden won the point and eventually the match. Pickard later said that he felt as sick as a pig.

9. *Pigs on the Wing*

Speaking of pigs, we flashback to the famous 'Battle of the Sexes' match in Houston, 1973. Billie Jean King was furious when 55-year-old Bobby Riggs defeated her 30-year-old rival, Margaret Court, and kept bragging that women had no chance against men in tennis. Billie Jean King took on Bobby Riggs, and as a crowd of 30,472 watched in the arena, as did 48 million Americans on television, Riggs made his arrival in a rickshaw pulled by six nymphets. Billie Jean King was carried to the tennis court on a litter and presented Riggs with a live piglet for his male chauvinistic ways. King also had the last laugh as she beat Riggs in straight sets.

8. *Battle of the Sex Change*

The 1977 US Open saw Renee Richards make her debut in women's Singles when she faced Virginia Wade. But there was a catch. Cut to 17 years earlier, when she, or rather he, had made his debut in the men's Singles at the 1960 US Open. Richard H. Raskind underwent a sex-change operation in 1975 and transformed into Renee Richards. But despite the desire to win, victory remained elusive, as Richard H. Raskind lost in the first round at the 1960 US Open and so did Renee Richards in the 1977 US Open.

7. *Wimbledon's Strict Dressing Rules Strike Again*

True to her name, American tennis player Anne White, as per convention, was dressed in all-white for the Wimbledon Championships in 1985. Well, not quite. White had chosen to play tennis in a skin-tight jumpsuit that the

Wimbledon organizers did not approve of. This outfit caused a stampede by the photographers as Miss White made her grand court entry. In fact, no one clicked her more celebrated opponent, Pam Shriver, at all. Ultimately, White was asked to wear something more conventional the next day. This must have done considerable damage to her spirits, as she lost the match after it was one-set all on the first day, before bad weather had suspended play.

6. *Moody Blues*

Cannes 1926 was quite the tennis spectacle as hundreds of fans queued all night outside the stadium, and the Train Blue that arrived from Paris was full of tennis fans. French diva Suzanne Lenglen faced the challenger American Helen Wills, and French fans were delighted when Lenglen prevailed after a tense finish to win the contest. As her fans carried Lenglen off the court, Wills stood sadly in the middle of the court all alone. She was comforted by a male fan, who joined her on court. 'You played awfully well,' the admirer, named Frederick Moody, said. Well, love is known to strike at the strangest places, and the tennis court is no exception. The two were married three years later, and Helen became Helen Wills-Moody, the name that fetched her great tennis fame later. She had just won 1 Grand Slam Singles title before her marriage, as Helen Wills. Post-marriage, she won a total of 31 Career Grand Slam titles, which included 19 Grand Slam Singles titles.

5. *The Angry Wife*

We all know how angry wives can get. But this one is a wild case for sure. American Jeff Tarango was a tennis

Helen Wills and Frederick Moody

player famous for flaring up faster than a forest fire. His wife, Benedicte, had the same characteristics and flipped faster than the meanest acrobat. At Wimbledon 1995, Tarango was playing a match against German Alexander Mronz. The Californian started arguing when what he thought was an ace was called out. When the crowd started booing him, Tarango told them to shut up, but in more unprintable words. The chair umpire, Bruno Rebeuh, issued a code violation to Tarango, which really made him lose his shirt. Jeff Tarango shouted at Rebeuh, calling him the most corrupt official he'd ever seen, and then walked off the court, defaulting the match to his opponent. As Rebeuh walked back to the changing room, he faced the wrath of the angry wife as Benedicte came up and slapped him. Later, Benedicte defended her strange action, saying that her husband would have been banned from tennis if he had slapped Bruno Rebeuh instead. Well, that makes sense. It takes two to Tarango!

4. *The Groundsman's Double Fault*

In a bizarre incident during a tennis match at Amelia Island in Florida in 2002, it was discovered that the groundsman had screwed up big time, as the Americans would put it. The groundsman, Bert Evatt, was understandably embarrassed as he admitted to having flip-flopped the distances from the net to the service line and then to the baseline. The normal distance is 21 feet from the net to the service line and then it is 18 feet to the baseline. The groundman had done the opposite, and for someone who had been a groundsman for 22 years, this error is quite baffling, unless he had changed what he was smoking or drinking. This discovery was made after the complaints made by tennis players Anne Kremer and Jennifer Hopkins to the officials. The two players served as many as 29 double faults in the first round of the prestigious Bausch & Lomb Championships, which was played on the wrongly measured stadium court. It's also bizarre how the officials made this startling discovery only after the complaints were made. There must be something in that Florida air!

3. *Bill N' Babe*

Wimbledon 1921 witnessed a strange final in which American Bill Tilden faced Brian 'Babe' Norton of South Africa. Tilden won this match and the title in a five-setter 4–6, 1–6, 6–1, 6–0, 7–5. Rumours suggested that Norton considered Tilden his mentor and could not bring himself to beat him. So, Norton was accused of throwing the match away. Tennis historian Ted Tinling wrote that many tennis greats and experts present at the match agreed that the result of the match was affected by a psychological relationship that was probably homosexual. If it's true, imagine throwing away a Wimbledon title for a mentor in today's times. Nah!

2. *The Romanian Fiasco*

The 1972 Davis Cup final between the USA and Romania, held in Bucharest, was weird in every sense of the word. The American players, led by Arthur Ashe, alleged that local officials cheated in an unimaginable way. The most controversial match among the five played was the five-setter where American Stan Smith beat Romanian Ion Țiriac. A high number of foot faults were called by the judges, who wanted to cut down Smith's aces, according to Arthur Ashe. Țiriac was also accused of instigating the partisan crowd to disturb Smith. But what really infuriated the American players was Țiriac's cramping leg being openly massaged by a Romanian linesman, who was supposed to be impartial. Doubling up as a masseur is the quality of a skilled linesman, though, especially in a country like Romania. But despite all the Romanian efforts, the United States won 3–2 to clinch their fifth consecutive Davis Cup title.

1. *To Bee Or Not To Bee*

The 2024 Indian Wells ATP tournament, now known as the BNP Paribas Open, witnessed a strange incident. There was a bee invasion on court, which stopped the proceedings of a match played between Carlos Alcaraz and Alexander Zverev for as long as two hours. The two players were forced to leave the court as a sizeable swarm of bees landed on Court 1 unannounced and without buying any tickets. These creatures were drawn to the Spidercam, the broadcast camera you see moving on a cable over the court. The vibrations from the Spidercam probably made the bees disoriented, which were initially attracted to their queen, who refused to move from the camera. All queens love the camera, after all, even if it's a Spidercam and a queen bee in question. Local beekeeper Lance Davis was summoned, and he proved his mettle by vacuuming the swarm of bees from the Spidercam without wearing a protective body suit. He's a true beekeeper, that man. After a long delay, the match finally resumed and was won by Alcaraz, who called it the most unusual match he'd ever played. But there always seems to be a buzz on court whenever Carlos Alcaraz is playing!

IMAGE COPYRIGHT INFORMATION

Page 9: Tennis Balls and Rackets: Photo by Abigail Sylvester: https://www.pexels.com/photo/tennis-rackets-and-balls-on-court-34015721/

Page 11: Björn Borg: Rob Croes / Anefo, CC BY-SA 3.0 NL <https://creativecommons.org/licenses/by-sa/3.0/nl/deed.en>, via Wikimedia Commons

Page 33: Dimensions of a Standard Tennis Court: Businns, CC BY-SA 4.0 <https://creativecommons.org/licenses/by-sa/4.0>, via Wikimedia Commons

Page 55: Wimbledon Logo: Daniel from Galashiels, United Kingdom, CC BY 2.0 <https://creativecommons.org/licenses/by/2.0>, via Wikimedia Commons

Page 66: Ball Boys and Girls at Wimbledon 2025: Partynia, CC BY 4.0 <https://creativecommons.org/licenses/by/4.0>, via Wikimedia Commons

Page 80: Roland-Garros Logo: Carine06 from UK, CC BY-SA 2.0 <https://creativecommons.org/licenses/by-sa/2.0>, via Wikimedia Commons

Page 85: William Renshaw and Ernest Renshaw: Public domain, via Wikimedia Commons

Page 88: Jacques-Brugnon Cup: Chabe01derivative work: Kacir, CC BY-SA 4.0 <https://creativecommons.org/licenses/by-sa/4.0>, via Wikimedia Commons

Page 98: Rolex at Roland-Garros: Rian (Ree) Saunders, CC BY 2.0 <https://creativecommons.org/licenses/by/2.0>, via Wikimedia Commons

Page 100: US Open Logo: Chermayeff & Geismar & Haviv, Public domain, via Wikimedia Commons

Page 103: Chris Evert: Original: Los Angeles Times / Derivative work: Danyele, CC BY 4.0 <https://creativecommons.org/licenses/by/4.0>, via Wikimedia Commons

Page 104: Jimmy Connors: Koen Suyk / Anefo, CC BY 4.0 <https://creativecommons.org/licenses/by/4.0>, via Wikimedia Commons

Page 106: Billie Jean King: Lynn Gilbert, CC BY-SA 4.0 <https://creativecommons.org/licenses/by-sa/4.0>, via Wikimedia Commons

Page 111: Martina Navratilova: Hans van Dijk for Anefo, CC0, via Wikimedia Commons

Page 116: John McEnroe: photograph by Rob C. Croes; crop by User:WolfRayet, CC BY-SA 3.0 <https://creativecommons.org/licenses/by-sa/3.0>, via Wikimedia Commons

Page 120: Gabriela Sabatini: United States Embassy to Argentina, Buenos Aires, CC BY 2.0 <https://creativecommons.org/licenses/by/2.0>, via Wikimedia Commons

Page 123: Australian Open Logo: Fetutxini31416, CC0, via Wikimedia Commons

Page 144: Rohan Bopanna: si.robi, CC BY-SA 2.0 <https://creativecommons.org/licenses/by-sa/2.0>, via Wikimedia Commons

Page 152: Steffi Graf: Mister-E (Chris Eason), CC BY 2.0 <https://creativecommons.org/licenses/by/2.0>, via Wikimedia Commons

Page 158: Davis Cup Trophy: Акутагава, CC BY-SA 3.0 <https://creativecommons.org/licenses/by-sa/3.0>, via Wikimedia Commons

Page 163: René Lacoste: Bundesarchiv, Bild 102-07746 / CC-BY-SA 3.0, CC BY-SA 3.0 DE <https://creativecommons.org/licenses/by-sa/3.0/de/deed.en>, via Wikimedia Commons

Page 164: Rod Laver: Evers, Joost / Anefo, CC0, via Wikimedia Commons

Page 168: Boris Becker: Flickr-User mandj98, CC BY 2.0 <https://creativecommons.org/licenses/by/2.0>, via Wikimedia Commons

Page 170: Jim Courier: ZankaM, CC BY-SA 3.0 <https://creativecommons.org/licenses/by-sa/3.0>, via Wikimedia Commons

Page 171: Andre Agassi: Xfranksun, CC BY 4.0 <https://creativecommons.org/licenses/by/4.0>, via Wikimedia Commons

Page 172: Roger Federer: Tatiana from Moscow, Russia, CC BY-SA 2.0 <https://creativecommons.org/licenses/by-sa/2.0>, via Wikimedia Commons

Page 173: Rafael Nadal: Carine06 from UK, CC BY-SA 2.0 <https://creativecommons.org/licenses/by-sa/2.0>, via Wikimedia Commons

Page 174: Novak Djokovic: Carine06 from UK, CC BY-SA 2.0 <https://creativecommons.org/licenses/by-sa/2.0>, via Wikimedia Commons

Page 176: Evonne Goolagong: Rob Mieremet / Anefo, CC0, via Wikimedia Commons

Page 177: Martina Hingis: si.robi, CC BY-SA 2.0 <https://creativecommons.org/licenses/by-sa/2.0>, via Wikimedia Commons

Page 179: Venus Williams: The Cosmopolitan of Las Vegas, CC BY-SA 2.0 <https://creativecommons.org/licenses/by-sa/2.0>, via Wikimedia Commons

Page 181: Monica Seles: Stacey Warnke from New Orleans, LA, CC BY-SA 2.0 <https://creativecommons.org/licenses/by-sa/2.0>, via Wikimedia Commons

Page 184: Margaret Court: Verhoeff, Bert / Anefo neg. stroken, 1945-1989, 2.24.01.05, item number 923-7057, CC BY-SA 3.0 NL <https://creativecommons.org/licenses/by-sa/3.0/nl/deed.en>, via Wikimedia Commons

Page 186: Serena Williams: Edwin Martinez from The Bronx, CC BY 2.0 <https://creativecommons.org/licenses/by/2.0>, via Wikimedia Commons

Page 192: Maria Sharapova: si.robi, CC BY-SA 2.0 <https://creativecommons.org/licenses/by-sa/2.0>, via Wikimedia Commons

Page 201: Leander Paes: si.robi, CC BY-SA 2.0 <https://creativecommons.org/licenses/by-sa/2.0>, via Wikimedia Commons

Page 202: Mahesh Bhupathi: Carine06, CC BY-SA 2.0 <https://creativecommons.org/licenses/by-sa/2.0>, via Wikimedia Commons

Page 203: Sania Mirza: Vinod Divakaran @ Doha Stadium Plus Qatar from Doha, Qatar, CC BY 2.0 <https://creativecommons.org/licenses/by/2.0>, via Wikimedia Commons

Page 221: Arthur Ashe: Bogaerts, Rob / Anefo, CC BY-SA 3.0 NL <https://creativecommons.org/licenses/by-sa/3.0/nl/deed.en>, via Wikimedia Commons

Page 253: Helen Wills and Frederick Moody: *Los Angeles Times*, CC BY 4.0 <https://creativecommons.org/licenses/by/4.0>, via Wikimedia Commons

INDEX